# A ROUND TO REMEMBER

Also by Michael McDonnell

*World of Golf Annual 1970–71*
*Golf: The Great Ones*
*Great Moments in Sport: Golf*
*Complete Book of Golf*

with Gary Player
*To be the Best: Gary Player*

# A ROUND TO REMEMBER

## MICHAEL MCDONNELL

# PARTRIDGE PRESS

LONDON · NEW YORK · TORONTO · SYDNEY · AUCKLAND

TRANSWORLD PUBLISHERS LTD
61-63 Uxbridge Road, London W5 5SA

TRANSWORLD PUBLISHERS (AUSTRALIA) PTY LTD
15-23 Helles Avenue, Moorebank, NSW 2170

TRANSWORLD PUBLISHERS (NZ) LTD
3 William Pickering Drive,
Albany, Auckland

Published 1992 by Partridge Press
a division of Transworld Publishers Ltd
Copyright © Michael McDonnell

A catalogue record for this book is available from the British Library
ISBN 185225 1476

Typeset in 10/12½ pt Plantin by
Falcon Graphic Art Ltd.
Printed in Great Britain by
Bath Press Colour Books, Glasgow

*For Michael, Jessica and Fiona*

My grateful thanks to Phil Sheldon who has supplied the majority of the photographs and who has been extremely helpful in the planning of this book.

I should also like to thank the *Daily Mail* library which has been a vital source of reference.

# CONTENTS

Behind every round of golf there is a story to be told. And behind some of the great rounds the narrative gets even better.

It is not just the merit of the performance itself – the skill, judgement and even courage required to excel – but rather the context in which it is achieved. In this sense it is the human predicament which is paramount and golf, though integral, becomes the backdrop.

It is a principle that applies across all aspects of the game and one I learned early in my journalistic career when I was obliged to collect competition scores from local golf clubs for a weekly newspaper. The figures were astronomical even after handicap deductions, but each winning round held its own drama, crisis, good fortune, momentary excellence – even courage – and when recounted afterwards made a rattling good tale.

It was one of the reasons I became a golf writer; I realized each round of golf was an adventure in itself with its own twists, turns and pitfalls. Moreover, it held all the pace and excitement of the more exhausting pursuits.

But when the game becomes the *raison d'être*, then its significance is overwhelming and when it is played to its highest limits on the great occasions, it stands for more than a demonstration of superior skill. In these circumstances a player is learning the truth about himself and almost certainly living through and conquering some personal crisis through his golf because it is so much part of his life.

This is the context in which the following stories have been told and the reason they have been chosen. They represent a crisis point – perhaps a pivotal moment – in each of the lives of the great contemporary players. In some cases I asked them to define their most important rounds. In others I made the choice.

In every case, the round meant something more than simply a tally of strokes. The background itself was all-important because such circumstances gave the performance its point, urgency and ultimate merit. All of them therefore carry the same theme: self-fulfilment and self-esteem through this extraordinary and capricious game.

In most cases they were all its victims in one way or another. Jack Nicklaus seemed to have grown too old. John Mahaffey was thwarted by failure. Bernhard Langer intimidated by a larger-than-life rival. Sandy Lyle robbed suddenly of his talent. And Greg Norman taunted by what might have been. Each had to recognize the personal demon and then overcome it in the only way possible – on a golf course and on the great occasion when nothing less would do.

This, then, is a tribute to such heroes of golf and an account of the most important rounds of their lives. Above all, these are human stories that reveal as much about the men themselves as their golf. That is another reason I took up golf writing all those years ago.

Michael McDonnell
Pleshey 1992

# CHAPTER ONE

# Tom Watson and the old gunslinger

It was the wrong scenario. There, sitting at the head of a large and boisterous dinner table was Big Jack, the loser. A few feet away over by the wall, sitting quietly with his wife, was Watson, the winner.

This was not how it should have been; or rather not how thousands of fans who, only a few hours earlier, had watched these great performers elevate the game of golf to new standards, would have imagined the backstage mood after one of the most momentous confrontations in sporting history.

It is said that rivalry in professional sport – especially between two gifted individuals – is the greatest spur and lifts each to levels of performance they never knew existed within themselves as they strive to beat each other.

That truth was to be found even in the restrained world of golf. For two glorious days during the 1977 Open championship at Turnberry, when Watson and Nicklaus realized the title rested between them, they had slugged it out with all the determination, fury and guile of heavyweight fighters.

But there was more than just an important title at stake as both men had known when they assembled on the first tee of the Ailsa Course. Both had joked that it was rather like a Western movie – Nicklaus, the old gunslinger, facing up to Watson, the new kid in town.

And beneath that lighthearted analogy lay a deeper suspicion that perhaps the Nicklaus Era was about to come to an end and that the Age of Watson had begun. Big Jack had said as much when he confessed, 'It was like that when I came on the scene. I knew Arnold Palmer was not going to give up easily. That made me play harder.'

True enough, Nicklaus had incurred the wrath of a million American fans as he toppled their beloved folk hero, Arnie. He had become the relentless target of hurtful campaigns from golf fans, including their awful practice of standing in the rough and holding up banners bearing the message: 'Hit it here, Fats!'

Nicklaus had confided to close friends that the more he was subjected to this form of attack, the more determined he was to prevail even though he was a close friend of Arnold Palmer and their personal

The Watson Era could not begin until the legend of Jack Nicklaus had been laid to rest. Both men knew this was the real reason for this historic showdown at Turnberry. *Phil Sheldon* competitiveness never went beyond the fairways.

While Big Jack eventually commanded huge respect for his achievements from the golfing public around the world, he accepted as a fact of life that he could not generate the warmth that had come so easily to Palmer. That, in turn, meant that no subsequent usurper would find himself the target of the kind of abuse that had been directed at Jack during his emerging days.

Yet, it was also clear that Watson, in a sense, was 'feeding' off him; had made him the target whenever they played to a point not too far short of obsession. There had been that extraordinary incident at Augusta earlier in the year when Watson was the only person present to mistake Nicklaus's triumphant punch after scoring a birdie as a personal and provocative gesture directed towards him.

It had happened on the fifteenth hole while Watson, waiting in the match behind to play his shot across the water, saw Nicklaus hole out then apparently turn back down the fairway and gesture in animated fashion. Watson admitted he was furious and that anger may have spurred him on to a scintillating finish in which he beat Nicklaus by a stroke for the title.

But then he seemed to realize that it had been outrageous to even think that Nicklaus would pull such a callous trick of gamesmanship and when Watson apologized Jack was even more surprised that anybody could ever believe he would need to resort to such tactics.

It had been an important victory for Watson because it ended speculation that he would be unable to handle the big moment under pressure. He had squandered two chances of US Open victory and even his 1975 Open triumph at Carnoustie was being dismissed as winning the easy way – by taking a play-off in which there was only one opponent, the Australian, Jack Newton, on whom to concentrate in what for practical terms had become pure matchplay.

Yet at Augusta, Watson had won in distinguished company and had tamed the Golden Bear who had been playing at his best in that last round with a 66. But it had still not been good enough and thoughts began to form that perhaps the new hero was about to set standards that would stretch beyond the reach of Nicklaus.

What was certain however was that Nicklaus himself would not give up without a fight and that if Watson was to be his successor then he would have to prove it conclusively by winning more than one championship title from Jack. Nobody doubted this truth as they arrived for the 1977 Open championship at Turnberry.

They could reflect on identical scores for three rounds, 68-70-65, that were to bring them together for this final day although their battle had commenced in the third round when they raced away from the rest of the field and into an incredible world of their own.

After four holes on that third day, they had four birdies between them and it was as though they had forgotten about the ranks of international superstars who had also gathered to play, nor were they worried or deflected from their brilliance by a thirty-minute delay for a thunderstorm as they marched over the Ailsa Course which was being used for the first time that year as an Open venue, to finish with 65 apiece and knowing they would still be locked in combat on the next day.

When their names were called to the tee, there was to be a taste of the great matches of the past when thousands would turn out to support their particular hero. Big Jack had joked that he wanted another 'notch on my gun' and the newspapers had reported it so that all the fans knew exactly how intense this duel was about to become.

In a sense Nicklaus caught his younger rival napping right at the start when he snapped up a birdie on the first hole to go one stroke ahead. It was to be a feature of this showdown that Watson found himself constantly obliged to make up ground, to hang on as Big Jack produced many of the early spectacular thrusts.

Watson was a curious contradiction. He was hailed as the new genial Huckleberry Finn character of American sport, and though he had a ready smile and an easy manner, there was a point beyond which he would not allow public and press to intrude. He did not fit the image of a cult-hero who has his own jet or a much-photographed luxury home. In fact, Watson refused to allow his home in Kansas City to be pictured nor would he be interviewed there.

It was as though he saw the need for division in his life, and that golf — even at the highest level — was simply a job of work. He possessed a substantial intellect and earned a psychology degree at the prestigious Stanford University in California without the need of a golf scholarship. In truth he had no reputation of note as an amateur golfer.

Yet he had now stepped into the role of new hero and had found himself in a face-to-face confrontation with the man he would have to defeat if he was to be taken seriously. Other victories had a sort of statistical merit about them whenever the two rivals were not paired together and could only match scores afterwards to see who was the better man. But this day, each man would see every move the other made; would learn from it, be intimidated by it, but perhaps inspired by it, too.

By the time they completed the fourth hole Nicklaus seemed to have stamped his mark on the title as he moved three strokes clear of a young rival who had not quite found his stride. But Nicklaus himself was too much of an old hand not to know that Watson could strike at any moment and in particular when he himself might have been tempted to feel he was cruising towards victory.

Big Jack was absolutely correct because without warning Watson erupted savagely with three birdies in succession for which he had no answer and which brought them back on level terms. As they marched over the fairways on the edge of Turnberry Bay with Ailsa Craig looming offshore in the distance, they were like a pair of pied pipers as fans deserted other matches and flocked to watch them in this titanic struggle.

There was an unspoken fear that the crowds were becoming too large and were

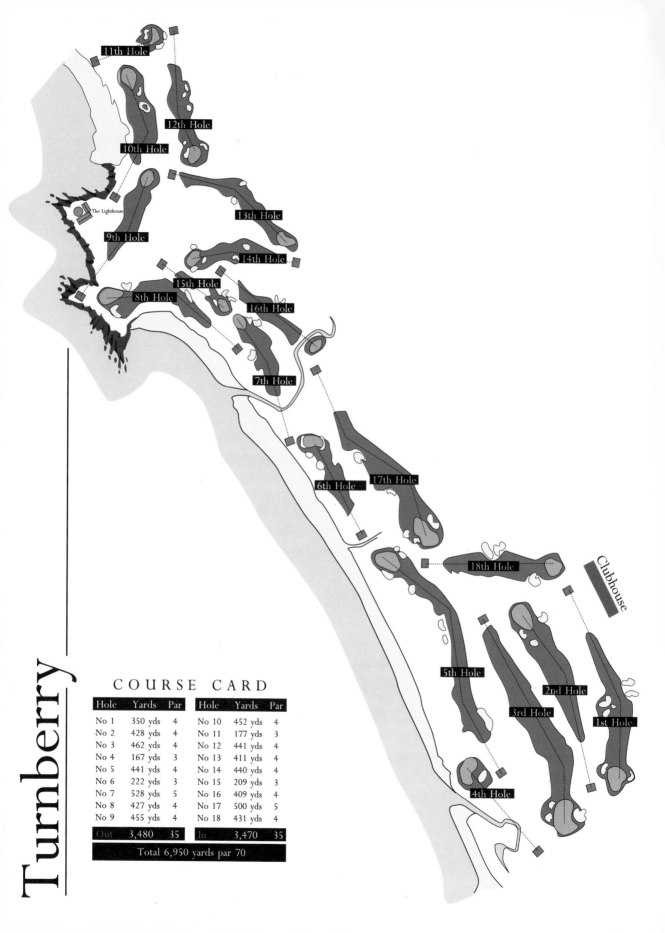

# Turnberry

11th Hole

12th Hole

10th Hole

The Lighthouse

9th Hole

13th Hole

14th Hole

15th Hole

8th Hole

16th Hole

7th Hole

6th Hole

17th Hole

18th Hole

Clubhouse

5th Hole

2nd Hole

3rd Hole

1st Hole

4th Hole

## COURSE CARD

| Hole | Yards | Par | Hole | Yards | Par |
|------|-------|-----|------|-------|-----|
| No 1 | 350 yds | 4 | No 10 | 452 yds | 4 |
| No 2 | 428 yds | 4 | No 11 | 177 yds | 3 |
| No 3 | 462 yds | 4 | No 12 | 441 yds | 4 |
| No 4 | 167 yds | 3 | No 13 | 411 yds | 4 |
| No 5 | 441 yds | 4 | No 14 | 440 yds | 4 |
| No 6 | 222 yds | 3 | No 15 | 209 yds | 3 |
| No 7 | 528 yds | 5 | No 16 | 409 yds | 4 |
| No 8 | 427 yds | 4 | No 17 | 500 yds | 5 |
| No 9 | 455 yds | 4 | No 18 | 431 yds | 4 |
| Out | 3,480 | 35 | In | 3,470 | 35 |

Total 6,950 yards par 70

Watson had already thwarted the Golden Bear to win the US Masters at Augusta earlier in the year. He was about to establish himself as the new dominant figure of the age. *Phil Sheldon*

not quite under control. Both Watson and Nicklaus sensed the dangers and in more practical terms told marshals they could no longer see the targets, particularly the bunkers, because the crowds were closing in on the edges of the fairways. The two men decided they would not play on until the crowds were moved back and under better control.

The delay and crisis seemed to have an unsettling effect on Watson who had just grabbed the initiative and had looked as though he was about to take command of the encounter. But Nicklaus stayed cool and was grateful to find himself with a one-stroke lead after nine holes, not through his own outstanding play but because of a Watson error.

Watson was still having trouble settling back to the task at hand and had to work overtime to save himself at the next two holes. He hit short into a bunker beside the tenth green yet played a superb recovery within a few feet of the hole to save par.

Nicklaus hit the next green and left his ball 12 feet from the hole and Watson could only toil for his par and breathe a sigh of relief when his rival missed the chance to increase his lead. Not that it mattered because Nicklaus completed that formality at the next green by holing from 25 feet.

This was the moment when it all seemed to be slipping away from Watson. Could he really give Jack Nicklaus a two-stroke advantage over the last six holes and still beat him? The idea seemed preposterous and perhaps it was wise of him not to think of the predicament in such depressing terms.

He knew he was running out of time and holes and that awareness gave his play the urgency it needed as he snapped back at Nicklaus's lead with a birdie on the thirteenth green to narrow the margin to one stroke. And there it was. A test of nerve over the closing stages of a world championship between a proven champion whose nerve remained cool and determined under the most extreme pressure and a young, still erratic talent, who had been known to fumble his chances.

There was much to be won and lost. Both had sensed beforehand that this show-down might well decide each of their destinies. For Watson, a new era or a false dawn? For Nicklaus, the end of it all or a reprieve until the next contender came along?

The question was, however, how many more challengers could Nicklaus dispatch before it really was time for him to be out-manoeuvred, or in Western parlance, out-gunned? There is a theory that at the very top level a man has a certain ration of nerve to withstand the pressures and that there comes a moment when it is all used up and no matter how well he can still strike a ball he is no longer a top-class competitor.

It had happened to the legendary Ben Hogan whose striking prowess had not diminished but who suddenly discovered he had lost his putting nerve and who would become transfixed over even the simplest putt until his arms and putter jumped into an unexpected spasm. The harsh reality was that his ration of nerve had gone and that all his experience of tension no longer toughened him but served only to punish him with memories of what could go wrong.

Nicklaus could look back on a succession of new challengers who had threatened to topple him but who, perhaps through his own skills as well as their various limitations, had slipped from the scene. Tony Jacklin, on the threshold of an international career, confessed he realized he could never be the world's best golfer once he was aware just how good Big Jack could play.

Johnny Miller had bounced on to the international stage in spectacular style and been hailed as the new hero but he too lived to his own set of priorities and never quite reached that level of enduring ability and stature with which it is necessary to play to earn a rightful place in this company.

But this Watson was rather different. He had Jack in his sights, not simply to do better than him but to beat him personally. And that was an altogether different situation for the older man to handle. It was one thing to be beaten but quite another to realize that by losing to Watson he himself enhanced the prestige and importance of the man's victory.

Yet, there was still that precious one-stroke advantage over Watson as they came to the fifteenth tee and looked towards the flag some 200 yards away. There was a mood of expectancy, an incredible moment when thousands fell silent waiting for the strike.

As soon as he hit, Watson knew that his ball was missing the green

on the left and it finished awkwardly in bumpy and miserable terrain. Nicklaus, the old professional, had obeyed the first rule of successful matchplay – never miss the green on the par threes – and was safely on the putting surface. The fans sensed the contest was taking an inevitable shape as the young man struggled.

By the time Watson reached the green and took out his putter just to nudge the ball on its near 40-yard journey so that it would trickle over the ground through the fringe to somewhere on the green, the knowing Scots shook their heads and assumed the best he could hope for was to get the ball close enough to save par. But that might still not be good enough with Nicklaus sitting with the chance of a birdie.

What happened next changed the course of the championship and golfing history. Watson nudged the ball into life and it bumped, this way and that, down the slope to the green then seemed to straighten up on a deadly course to hit the flagstick and disappear from view. It had been a stunning stroke. It had earned him a birdie and flabbergasted Big Jack.

When the roars had died, Nicklaus crouched over the putt in his old familiar style but his customary resolve had gone. He was a man imitating himself, he had not really tuned in to the task. The ball missed. He had taken a par and they were on level terms when minutes earlier it had seemed he would race away with it.

It had been a lethal blow and, although nobody saw him actually shake his head to think clearly again, he coiled the swing

# A ROUND TO REMEMBER

Both men were so concerned that the huge crowd might get out of control.  They could no longer see the targets and refused to play on until the marshals took effective action. *Phil Sheldon*

into action from the next tee and was on the green across the treacherous and deep burn that flows out to sea in two shots. Watson gave him just a faint hope when his own approach to the green came up crucially short and perched on the edge of the long horrible slope into the burn.

The fans waited to see if the ball had stuck fast or whether it would suddenly begin to roll back down gaining sickening momentum as it went. But it stayed and if Watson felt like running to play the stroke before the ball moved he resisted the urge. Instead he chipped close and holed out for a par four.

They were still level as they clambered to the tee of the long seventeenth. Both were perfectly placed in the fairway but Nicklaus had just edged past his young rival with the driver. Thus Watson had to play first and it was to be a vital advantage as he rifled a two iron into the green. The waiting crowd was ecstatic.

It is a common practice among pros to learn how to judge the roar of a crowd – the pitch, strength, crescendo, length and volume all tell quite accurately the fate of the shot; the difference between the ball that ran close and missed, the one that finished reasonably well, the one that hit the hole and ran on and the one that actually dropped. The sounds of that Turnberry roar that day suggested that Watson was terribly, terribly close.

And Nicklaus responded. Or rather the obligation to get his own approach just as close became overwhelming. What emerged was a stroke that owed its weakness to the enormity of the pressure. The ball was hit 'fat'; he had committed the basic error of hitting the ground behind the ball – a duffer's mistake – and therefore had not imparted as much power as he knew he needed.

As a result the ball came up short and when he reached the green he realized that Watson's approach had not been so breathtakingly close but had finished 15 feet away – hardly a gimme putt for an eagle three. He returned to play his own chip shot and left the ball reasonably close. Watson missed his eagle and now Jack had this putt to stay on level terms as they went to the final hole in what had been a momentous encounter.

He knew the ball would take the slope from the right-hand side into the hole and that he must aim on that side and let it fall. It needed both pace and line to be absolutely precise on this kind of stroke. As he touched the ball into life, he knew the line was perfect but then he knew all at once that the pace was far too strong. Nicklaus and his fans knew the ball would not take the curve into the hole. Instead it stayed on the right-hand side and missed the target. He was one stroke behind.

Watson stepped up and drilled a long iron down the last fairway. Nicklaus reached for his driver in a move that mystified those around him because even if he hit the perfect stroke he would still be 140 yards from the green while Watson from his own tee shot had about 178 yards left to play; hardly a massive advantage and given the risks involved, particularly with the bushes and scrub flanking the right-hand side of the fairway, Nicklaus's choice did not seem worth it.

True enough, he cut his tee shot to

the base of some bushes and while he was sizing up how to play the stroke, indeed if there was one to be played, Watson, farther from the green, played a seven iron within 2 feet of the hole. Nobody doubted that Nicklaus could now be written off.

Yet some fierce pride still prompted Nicklaus to fight on. Perhaps too there was anger at himself at having succumbed to the pressure now and on the previous hole. He jabbed the ball clear to the front of the green but was still 35 feet from the hole.

The customary script at times like this in the closing moments of a great championship is for the emerging champion to be beyond dispute so that he can wave in triumph as he marches between the grandstands and on to glory. But this moment was bizarre. Nobody thought for one moment that Watson would miss from 2 feet. Nobody really believed that Nicklaus could hole his putt. And yet . . .

Both were cheered as they came to the last green. Nicklaus assessed his putt, marched round it, viewed it, then crouched over the ball. His caddie Jimmy Dickinson stood holding the flag and then removed it as soon as Nicklaus nudged the ball on its route. Up in the Turnberry Hotel they could hear the gathering roar as the ball moved closer, and closer, and closer, then disappeared into the hole for a staggering birdie three.

The cheers had not subsided when Watson replaced his ball, picked up his marker, stood over his own putt and rammed home the ball with his characteristic stiff-wristed jab to become champion – and so much more.

For the second time, he had beaten the great man at his very peak. He had removed all doubts about his own ability to win under pressure. Moreover he had lifted himself into the exclusive echelon of players whose careers are preoccupied with major titles. The Watson era had truly begun but it had needed this triumph over the greatest player of the previous generation to mark its arrival almost as a ritual.

They walked from the green arm-in-arm, growing in respect, esteem and warmth for each other. But that evening up at the hotel restaurant, Watson was subdued while Nicklaus entertained his family and friends. Perhaps it was precisely what both needed. When Big Jack had lost the 1972 Open at Muirfield by a stroke and with it the chance to hold all four major titles at the same time – he was to be found playing tennis at his hotel within the hour, because he 'needed to let off steam'.

It was no use dwelling on what might have been or what should have happened. It was time to celebrate and move on. And Watson? Perhaps the thought had just occurred to him of what he had done and what lay ahead; and that from now on, he would be the old gunslinger and the target for any kid of ambition who came to town.

# CHAPTER TWO

# Ian Woosnam and a score to settle

The note was waiting for him when he reached the locker-room. It was from his father. As Ian Woosnam read the words, it was as though all that had transpired until this moment had been part of the pilgrimage for the old man too.

If fathers really do seek fulfilment through their sons and for triumphs that somehow they themselves missed, then what was about to take place over West Course at Wentworth in the World Matchplay championship was as much a test for Harold Woosnam as it was for his son.

This was the moment that had been waiting for them; when both would discover whether the dreams and sacrifices, the setbacks, the false starts, the glimmers of glory had any cohesive point of destiny about them at all.

Father and son would both be locked in the drama and tension of this day and for every inch of the way – Harold outside the ropes and Ian on the fairways, untouchable, beyond paternal help as he faced the most important task of his professional career.

Both of them would know by nightfall if the substance of greatness was within Ian or whether neither could take his ability and skills even half-seriously again.

There was heavy symbolism about the moment as Ian considered his opponent. In essence Sandy Lyle epitomized all that he had struggled against from his boyhood days through the fruitless years of professional golf and now as he stood on the threshold of taking his place at the feast.

In a perverse way, Lyle had been the unwitting inspiration for all of this; not simply the target of his ambition nor the yardstick by which he could judge his own efforts but also the reason he had struggled against all the odds for so long.

This was a crusade that had begun in boyhood. It was also a score that Ian had to settle not merely on a personal basis – although there was that to it – but rather as the golden chance to redress the unfairness of those early years and the arbitrary manner in which fate had showered one of them with the priceless gifts while apparently short-changing the other.

Not simply physical size of course.

The World Matchplay final at Wentworth in 1987 and the moment for which Woosnam had waited a lifetime. At last he had the chance to prove himself against his childhood rival, Sandy Lyle. *Phil Sheldon*

# A ROUND TO REMEMBER

Even as fresh-faced kids in the Shropshire Boys team they were unmistakable. But little Ian ( sitting, 2nd from left ) judged himself against the exploits of big Sandy (standing, 2nd from left ) and was determined to catch up one day.
*Shropshire Star Newspaper*

# Wentworth

10th Hole

9th Hole

12th Hole

13th Hole

11th Hole

7th Hole

8th Hole

14th Hole

6th Hole

5th Hole

15th Hole

4th Hole

16th Hole

17th Hole

3rd Hole

2nd Hole

1st Hole

18th Hole

## COURSE CARD

| Hole | Yards | Par | Hole | Yards | Par |
|------|-------|-----|------|-------|-----|
| No 1 | 471 yds | 4 | No 10 | 186 yds | 3 |
| No 2 | 155 yds | 3 | No 11 | 376 yds | 4 |
| No 3 | 452 yds | 4 | No 12 | 483 yds | 5 |
| No 4 | 501 yds | 5 | No 13 | 441 yds | 4 |
| No 5 | 191 yds | 3 | No 14 | 179 yds | 3 |
| No 6 | 344 yds | 4 | No 15 | 466 yds | 4 |
| No 7 | 399 yds | 4 | No 16 | 380 yds | 4 |
| No 8 | 398 yds | 4 | No 17 | 571 yds | 5 |
| No 9 | 450 yds | 4 | No 18 | 502 yds | 5 |
| Out | 3,361 | 35 | In | 3,584 | 37 |
| | | Total 6,945 yards par 72 | | | |

Clubhouse

Ian never raged at his own diminutive 5 feet 4 inch stature. Nor could he blame Sandy for being 6 feet 1 inch. If anything, being short had made him compulsively assertive to the point of aggression, as well as quite fearless both on and off the fairways.

Life, from the earliest days on his father's farm at Oswestry, had been one sustained personal test in which every aspect had to be proved, or rather Ian himself had to show that being short made little difference to his wider abilities. Harold saw to that.

The tractor pedals were fitted with wooden blocks so that the boy Ian could reach them. He was not spared any of the burdensome tasks on the Woosnam farm which lay in the Shropshire countryside as it meets the Welsh borders.

It was Harold who pushed him into those junior boxing contests whenever they took a summer break at holiday camps. Even the larger lads had been taken aback and bloodied by the vehemence of Ian's attack. In the end nobody would fight him – except the trainer who knelt down to make a fairer fight of it.

There was, too, the occasional skirmish out of the ring whenever Ian felt he was somehow being pushed aside. Indeed, this compulsion to retaliate, to assert himself as forcefully as he could, would pursue him into adulthood with some damaging results.

And then there was Sandy. It had all been so different for him. The textbook success story. Born to golf at Hawkstone Park where his father, Alex, was professional. He had only to fall out of bed to

step on to a golf course and he could do so with constant paternal guidance and permission whenever he wished.

Not so Ian. For a start the golf course was on the other side of town and that meant a bike ride with clubs across the handle bars. And even then there could be no prospect of playing golf until all the jobs for the day on the farm had been completed.

They had been born within fourteen miles of each other in Shropshire. Ian was the elder by little over two months. They had been aware of each other of course throughout their junior days in county golf although there was no doubt that Sandy by common consent was regarded as one of the most gifted youngsters of his time. His talent was prodigious and natural, and he took it for granted.

Not so Ian. A good player of course, but self-made and successful only by dint of sheer hard work and determination. For him, it seemed success at golf would always be a struggle against his own inadequacies.

Lyle had noticed that truth with unintentional cruelty when both had reached the final of the Shropshire and Hereford Boys championship at Market Drayton. They were both twelve years old and Ian had lost to Sandy. He turned to the all-conquering Lyle and said, 'One day I'll beat you.'

Lyle had retorted, 'You'll have to grow a bit first, Woosie!' And now the day had arrived. He was about to confront Sandy in the final of a championship that had never been won by a home-based player in its history and in which Sandy had figured in three finals.

The note from Harold had reminded Ian of that vow he had made all those years ago when he lost the boys' championship at Market Drayton. In all honesty he had never envied the success of others but rather wondered what difference existed between them and himself.

No, it was more specific than that. He knew that he could strike the ball as far as any of the giants. All those years of working on the farm had endowed him with enormous strength quite out of proportion to his stature. It had not all been accidental of course because he had spent hours deliberately hitting golf balls out of long grass just to develop the strength in his arms.

He had to accept philosophically that doors would open for obviously talented individuals like Sandy while he would have to earn his keep. That was how it had been when he was obliged to strike a bargain with a nearby golf club – he would work behind the bar and as a part-time greenkeeper in return for a chance to practise and play the course on a regular basis.

But the art of successful golf at a professional level had eluded him and while Sandy soared towards stardom in easy contrast, he fought a constant battle with failure.

The dream had been that he would become the best golfer in the world. It filled him and yet there was no evidence to support the notion. Indeed as the weeks dragged into months and years, his personal record and bank balance showed precisely the opposite value on his talents.

He seemed at best a young man of defined sporting ability who would eventually realize his limitations and, once the wild oats had been sown, settle down to the cosy job as a club professional perhaps somewhere back in his native Shropshire where he was known.

In truth, his entire lifestyle in those early times had been a constant struggle simply to maintain his place on the European professional circuit. He failed three times and was obliged to re-qualify before he was safely if unspectacularly launched.

These were the wild times when he lost sight of his ambition because of the compelling evidence of failure before him and opted instead for the boisterous social life on tour somehow ignoring that self-defeating point of it all, the late nights and the drink merely guaranteeing even worse results on the golf course which in turn prompted even more refuge from reality in the high life. And so on.

And yet the irony was that part of the problem had been his compulsion to succeed and his obsession to hit only perfect shots; or rather to believe that he needed to play flawlessly to play successfully. It was of course a fallacy that he had not yet come to understand.

There was within him a fierce streak of independence. He would achieve success and accept it on his own terms. He lived on the breadline, driving to tournaments in a battered caravanette in which he lived and ate his daily ration of chips, crisps and hamburgers. By the time he had spent four seasons on tour, he had earned less than £2,000.

That year Sandy was third leading money winner in European golf with more than £50,000 to his credit as well as eight titles already to his name. The gulf between them was so enormous they might as well have been playing a different game.

Yet it is an extraordinary aspect of golf itself that the unexpected is always an even bet; that the predictable can be dubious and that even the seemingly most hopeless case hides the ingredients for a compelling success story.

In the early weeks of 1982, Ian had scraped together enough cash to finance a package tour round the African countries on the Safari Tour. One day on the eve of the Nigerian Open, it so happened he had found himself standing on the practice ground next to the slow, deliberate Yorkshireman Gordon Brand.

While Ian drilled the ball with relentless accuracy into the far distance, the man next to him seemed to be a comedy of errors – one ball over the fence, another scuffed 50 yards along the ground. Yet Brand was a proven money winner, a good commercial player who never left a tournament without a handsome cheque in his pocket even if it was never as the winner.

For Brand, the living was, if not easy, then at least attainable enough for him to support a wife and family and sustain a small farm in Ilkley. Yet for Woosnam, there was still not enough cash for him to even think about marrying Glendryth his childhood sweetheart who had gone to London to train as a nurse.

When the first round of the Nigerian Open had been completed Ian had scored a moderate 78. He looked at the leaderboard and was shocked to discover Brand – the man who had hit the ball all over the place in practice – had taken 68.

Suddenly the secret of it all hit him. The Yorkshireman was not the least bothered about his bad strokes. All that concerned him was his score and how to make it in whatever manner possible. There was no anguish – no heartache – over a poorly struck shot. The only obligation was to find the ball, forget about the error and hit it properly this time.

Truly there was no point in worrying about what had passed, particularly as such turmoil led Woosnam to bouts of club throwing and tantrums which themselves were self-defeating and self-perpetuating.

That was it. Trust the swing and just think about the score whatever way it happened. There could be no other way in a sport that gave such a harsh daily judgement on one's worth in terms of the score achieved.

How else was it to be managed – this constant pass-or-fail lifestyle that depended on the number of strokes taken to hit a ball cross-country every day of his life? It was a truth that others had learned and now it had come to him.

Later on, it was impossible to determine whether that realization had brought about instant transformation. Yet it was a matter of historical record that he picked up a car for a hole-in-one prize that week that was to boost

No crisis, not even a precarious stance on the edge of a bunker, would foil Woosnam's chance of victory that afternoon at Wentworth in the World Matchplay final. He had waited too long for this success. *Allsport*

his personal finances for the rest of the season.

By the end of the year, the tide of fortune had truly turned in his favour. He broke clear to win his first tour event as he became European Masters champion. Woosnam, it seemed, had at last found his stride as well as that essential blend of self-knowledge and technical consistency from which all successful golf must flow.

The money was no longer a problem now that he too could be guaranteed a handsome cheque every week that he played. Moreover, he felt confident enough to ask Glendryth to marry him and they went back to settle in their home town.

Glendryth had played a major role in his path to success and much more than anybody except the two of them would ever know. Perhaps it was the thought that he might lose her if he did not find some direction to his life through golf that prompted him to look for a way to succeed.

It was a stark choice. An aimless almost self-destructive life on tour among the supporting acts. Or, the prospect of a meaningful life with Glendryth if only he could fulfil his potential.

Now it had happened and in the intervening four years he had become a top earner and a performer regarded as a major attraction on any bill, although not yet top of that bill. Woosnam added essential edge to the cast of characters in which the likes of Seve Ballesteros, Nick Faldo, Sandy Lyle and Bernhard Langer were the names in bigger print.

Was he just a journeyman? Or was

there more to the career of Ian Woosnam? As he walked to the first tee of the West Course, nobody doubted that this was the moment in which he would find out whether he had the stature of a champion; whether he could withstand the pressures to take a prize that, quite apart from its intrinsic merit, would determine his claims to qualify as one of the best players in the world.

More than this, he had to prove himself against Sandy Lyle, whose erratic brilliance would be a major factor during the rest of the day because he was most lethal when he seemed most docile and defeated. In truth, it was about to be a long hard day for both of them.

Even so, Woosnam slipped comfortably into an early lead and Sandy seemed to be engrossed in getting both the measure of the course and his opponent. The crowd began to increase as they moved deeper into the country on the outward nine.

Woosnam was heartened to have Phil Morbey – Wobbly, they called him, because of the way he walked – at his side. The man knew his golf and more importantly knew Ian's golf and was absolutely accurate when it came to putting the correct club into Ian's hands. Before the day was out he would impose his will – when asked – several times on Woosnam when it came to a discussion over the choice of club. Ian knew the man was right.

Morbey had, after all, brought Ian this far against some of the strongest opposition ever to assemble in world golf. Woosie, the hero, had dismissed them all in a series of extraordinary struggles.

He had toppled Nick Faldo in an exhaustive encounter which endured until the last green when Ian found himself standing over a putt of no more than 6 feet for victory and without hesitation had dismissed the big man from the championship before shaking him by the hand. There had always been a genuine warmth of spirit between these two and a mutual, if unspoken, professional admiration.

Then it was the turn of Seve Ballesteros to discover he no longer had a place in the contest when, once again, Woosnam holed a winning putt of similar distance on the last green for victory and a place in the final. Some observers argued that Woosnam had already done enough to prove his worth in the best of company. And yet Lyle remained, and was waiting for him.

The morning round had an almost rhythmic pattern as Woosnam took a two-hole lead, was brought back, regained it and then lost and regained it twice more before reaching the long fifteenth. It was here that the apparently docile Lyle struck with sudden and venomous accuracy, and by the time Woosnam missed a putt from 4 feet on the long seventeenth hole round the corner by the splendid gardens of imposing residences, they were all square.

There was more trouble for Woosnam as Sandy ran down a putt from almost 20 feet for a devastating eagle three while he missed from a shorter distance. The man who had been cruising comfortably with a two-hole lead was suddenly trailing by a hole with the afternoon session still to be played.

'I'll beat you one day, Lyle.'

'You'll have to grow a bit first, Woosie.'

Just fine words? Or a prophecy?

For most of the lunch break Woosnam practised his putting stroke on the green outside Bernard Gallacher's pro shop. No point in getting angry with the technique. That, after all, had to be trusted. The game was about scores; as Walter Hagen had said, 'It's not "How", it's "How many."'

And yet Woosnam sensed there was something wrong with his putting stroke or rather that he did not feel comfortable as he stood over the ball. He was not settled and he did not know the reason.

In fact, come the afternoon round, the putting practice seemed to have been a waste of time when he missed a miserable little putt from 2 feet on the sixth green to hand a surprised and grateful Lyle an unexpected two-hole lead.

Woosnam did not know how it happened but in a moment of random adjustment as he tried to find a more comfortable stance over his putts, he stood more upright and suddenly felt as though all his posture was in proper position.

At the time he was 12 feet from the hole and desperately struggling to save himself sliding three down and virtually handing over all the initiative and advantage to Lyle. Even so, he decided it was time to try standing tall no matter what the outcome. He touched the ball into motion then glanced out of the corner of his eye as it ran towards the hole and disappeared for the vital half he needed.

Two holes later he stunned Lyle when he holed from 40 feet for a birdie to claw back some of his rival's lead. Without warning it had become the furious stuff of man-to-man conflict; as bruising in its own way as any heavyweight contest in the ring.

In truth, Woosnam sensed he had his man on the ropes as he snapped up a birdie on the short tenth hole over the trees with a putt from 2 feet to level their match.

This now was the moment. Perhaps the crowd sensed it too. There was more at stake than simple cash and glory. What made the trophy so important was that each knew the other wanted it and had to be stopped at all costs. Both knew that one false move could decide it.

That suspicion was to become agonizing fact for Lyle when, minutes later, the pressure began to assail his sure touch and he hooked a four iron approach over the green and lost his confident feel around it, taking three more strokes to hole out.

Woosnam was back in the lead but not for long because Lyle instantly regained his composure with a birdie on the sixteenth to level the match. Both men knew they were fast running out of holes.

The urgency tightened as they matched each other stroke for stroke as if more concerned with commendable caution than taking the risk of a bigger stroke in the hope of breaking the deadlock.

Woosnam thought he might have struck the winner on the long seventeenth when he deposited an obedient wedge shot 2 feet from the hole. But Sandy struck from 60 yards and left his golf ball 4 feet from the hole to save himself with the putt.

And so they came to the last hole; the climax of a lifetime's crusade for one man. Mercifully this was not a moment to dwell on the enormity of it all. For Woosnam, he could not only level that boyhood score with Sandy by depriving him of a great prize but, in so doing, could also establish himself as a player of true class.

Both blasted into play and when they reached their golf balls, Woosnam was pleased to see that he had first shot at the green because Sandy had just out-driven him.

In such moments there is no time to consider the list of horrors that could happen. The tightrope walker looks at the thickness of the rope, not the height of the drop should he miss. So it was with Woosnam as he reached into the bag for his three wood.

Without fuss or ritual, the crisp compact swing moved into lazy but positive action and the ball fizzed into the air on its 245-yard journey to the green. It was still airborne as the crowds realized it was on course and that it had the power to reach its target.

As it came to earth, the roars erupted as Woosnam knew they would. He also knew that Sandy's stroke had suddenly become an awesome prospect in the knowledge of how close to the flag his diminutive rival had deposited the ball.

Lyle reached for his two iron and knew that the best ploy was to aim on the right-hand bunker and hit the ball with enough right-to-left draw for it to drift back into the heart of the green.

The ball took flight on perfect line but suddenly Lyle realized there was something wrong and it was not moving back to its target but instead was staying suicidally on course for the bunker.

By the time he reached the trap he knew that at best he would have to rely on an error from Woosnam if this match was to go to extra holes. Sandy recovered well enough from the sand and for a moment there was obvious doubt about Woosnam's next move.

Should he fearlessly perform the *coup de grâce* and try to hole his putt for an eagle three and heroic triumph? But what if he ran the putt too far past and Sandy then holed his own putt? Supposing he then missed? What a disaster. Better to settle surely for two putts and a birdie and allow Sandy to take the chance.

Such calculations served only to leave the approach putt 6 feet short of the hole. If Sandy holed then the entire scenario would have lurched crazily in a matter of seconds and Ian, on the threshold of victory, would find himself on the defensive. But Sandy did not hole. Worse still in professional terms, he left the putt short.

Now it was Woosnam's turn as he faced a putt similar in length to those with which he had dismissed Ballesteros and Faldo in previous matches and on the same green too.

At such moments, the merciful repetition of a practised routine diminishes – or at least hides – the fear of failure and its awful consequences. No time to think about it. Just time to check the blade is square to the target; that the line is right, that the body is locked so it cannot sway and, above all, the pace is perfect to take the gentle slopes into the hole.

Then it was on its way. And suddenly it had disappeared. Woosnam was champion and so much more besides. Wobbly hugged him. Sandy came over and shook his hand. At last the old score had been settled even if it had taken Woosnam eighteen years to do it. But then it had never really been personal.

In the crowd, there was a diminutive Welsh farmer who was alone with his own thoughts. Harold Woosnam could not reach Ian even if he tried. There were too many officials and guards in the way. There would be interviews and speeches for the boy to make.

In any case, neither was too good at showing his feelings especially where each other was concerned, despite their deep affection. They both knew what this moment meant; how it signified Woosnam's elevation to the rare echelons of golf from which only champions emerge. And what gave them both hope as they celebrated in their own ways was the knowledge that the best was yet to come.

# CHAPTER THREE

# Seve Ballesteros and the things his father taught him

For a moment, it seemed as though his father had become the champion as the press crowded round him and, through an interpreter, he told them how important this triumph had been in the greater scheme of things.

But then Seve could not deny the old man his share of reflected glory, because he had played his part in this success, not in specific terms that week at Augusta but in ways that he would never know and in ways that even Seve himself could not define.

He had been the same towering hero figure to all his four sons. Big Baldomero, always smoking, had been the local hero in the village of Pedrena across the bay from Santander where the King of Spain built his summer palace.

He epitomized all the admirable qualities of courage, strength, skill and indomitable determination particularly when he took his place in the village rowing boat for the annual race of the *traineras* in the treacherous and deep waters of the bay.

Small wonder that Carmen Sota, daughter of a local farmer and sister of the local club professional, fell for him. And when their sons were born there was an inevitability that they too would be expected to demonstrate all the prowess and heroism he had possessed.

Not that it could ever work out like that. Baldomero, their eldest, was the protective one, always pensive, always careful for the others and, because he was the first-born, closest to, and perhaps intimidated by, the awesome example of his father.

Manuel was different. There was a wordliness, a personal toughness of spirit, that was absent from his elder brother. Of all the brothers, he was to be the driving force, the man who would urge them to carry on – to take that one last gasp when they felt like giving up.

Then came Vicente, the most subdued of them all; at times, it seemed, still looking for a personal role within their little group. Even in the famous years when the name of Ballesteros would symbolize golf, Vicente would remain the mystery man to the outside world.

The youngest of them all was Severiano and if the older boys looked to the standards set by their father and tried to keep pace, then young Seve was obliged also

It was always a personal battle between Seve and Augusta in which his rivals were forgotten and left far behind. Even a diversion into a sand trap could not halt his confident march to the 1983 US Masters title. *Phil Sheldon*

# Augusta

## COURSE CARD

| Hole | Yards | Par | Hole | Yards | Par |
|------|-------|-----|------|-------|-----|
| No 1 | 400 yds | 4 | No 10 | 485 yds | 4 |
| No 2 | 555 yds | 5 | No 11 | 455 yds | 4 |
| No 3 | 360 yds | 4 | No 12 | 155 yds | 3 |
| No 4 | 205 yds | 3 | No 13 | 465 yds | 5 |
| No 5 | 435 yds | 4 | No 14 | 405 yds | 4 |
| No 6 | 180 yds | 3 | No 15 | 500 yds | 5 |
| No 7 | 360 yds | 4 | No 16 | 170 yds | 3 |
| No 8 | 535 yds | 5 | No 17 | 400 yds | 4 |
| No 9 | 435 yds | 4 | No 18 | 405 yds | 4 |
| Out | 3,465 | 36 | In | 3,440 | 36 |

Total 6,905 yards par 72

Clubhouse

1st Hole
2nd Hole
3rd Hole
4th Hole
5th Hole
6th Hole
7th Hole
8th Hole
9th Hole
10th Hole
11th Hole
12th Hole
13th Hole
14th Hole
15th Hole
16th Hole
17th Hole
18th Hole

to live by the values and targets they set and expected him to observe without any fraternal compassion.

In a sense their personal values and worth became more clearly identified when all of them took up golf and followed it as a profession. The reason initially was simple enough: none was brilliantly gifted in the academic sense; all had inherited their father's athleticism and love for the outdoor life; and nearby – no more than a few hundred yards below their small farmhouse – lay the Royal Pedrena Golf Club where their uncle Ramon Sota was professional.

Ramon had been a player of considerable ability during the 1950s and 1960s, whose professionalism and experience had been his greatest qualities in helping him to several tournament victories.

Yet he presented a forbidding and almost repressive figure to his nephews when they turned up first to work as caddies and later as young professionals. His attitude was disparaging, perhaps intentionally so, because he knew how difficult it could be to sustain a lifestyle as a playing professional and how much heartbreak was involved.

To some extent his strategy was correct in that the brothers were obliged to be honest with themselves and examine their own abilities. In the fullness of time, Baldomero the Younger and Vicente would settle as club professionals; Manuel maintained a reasonable living on the playing circuit without major success before he too moved to a club job.

And yet Manuel possessed a shrewd professional judgement and recognized staggering talent when he saw it; and there it was in abundance in his little brother. This was no filial bias. This was a reality. The boy had an awareness – an understanding – of golf that surpassed anything he had ever seen.

It was as though all the father's great personal qualities had come together in Seve and manifested themselves in his instinctive ability to play golf. Most assuredly, he would need all those inherited strengths because the sport, at its highest level and in moments of intense drama, demands as much physical skill and courage as that needed to pull a *trainera* through the rolling waves of Santander Bay.

Golf itself had presented Seve with another, perhaps even greater, battle to fight and one that was to strike at the fundamental social structures into which Spain was then locked. He had chosen to excel in a sport which was trapped by a rigid class system; it was played by the very rich and its professionals came from the caddie classes.

The division was secure and unshakeable with the professional, though valued, never allowed to forget his place in this master-servant relationship. It had meant that golf for Seve – and in particular his clear genius at it – had to be used to contest wider issues and in the process the game itself was to become a crusade wherever he played.

Even this week at Augusta, there had been a compulsion to prove a point through his golf. He had already won the title and he had won the British

# A ROUND TO REMEMBER

From his father, Baldomero, he had inherited both powerful courage and physique. Both men loved to spend time together in a boat on Santander Bay where the old man had once been a champion rower. *Neville Marriner/Solo*

What remained was the simple formality of winning the 1983 title at Augusta once he had contained the crisis on the final day. It was his third major title and lifted him among the ranks of truly great players. *Phil Sheldon*

Open. Yet he sensed there was still a doubt about his worth, particularly by Americans who had dismissed his 1979 win at Royal Lytham and St Annes as sheer good fortune.

Someone cruelly branded him as the car-park champion, because he had played a recovery stroke from beside some parked cars to win the title. What they had failed to realize was that Seve savoured such outrageously difficult strokes.

He had passed endless hot, dusty afternoons in his boyhood waiting around the caddie shed for a bag to carry, by playing the most contrived recovery shots for a few pesetas against his young colleagues. He rarely lost.

In truth, those were not lucky strokes; they defined an uncanny almost instinctive notion of what a golf ball could, and would, do; those escape shots required as much supreme ball skill as any displayed by a great footballer. Moreover, they were the strokes that pleased him when he had time to reflect upon them later.

A psychologist might find some deeper reason for the combative use to which Seve put golf, using it as a weapon to get on even terms with people he sensed were against him. It was as though there had to be some anger within him, or some target for it, before he could resort to his best play.

Perhaps it was just a matter of fierce pride rather than that he was the intended target for the insults he thought were being directed towards him; maybe too it was his refusal to conform that brought him into such regular conflict with players and officials.

He considered that he had a special 'destino', and spoke freely of it even though such uninhibited admissions did not strike a sympathetic chord with some of his fellow professionals, nor did the actions which stemmed from his view of life fit easily with the code of professional golf around the world.

At times he was a man in conflict with, it seemed, almost everybody. He had been dropped from the European Ryder Cup team when clearly he was the best player, apparently because, in direct contravention of the regulations, he insisted on taking appearance money from sponsors to turn up and play.

He was to find himself outlawed by American officialdom because he insisted on the freedom to play wherever he wanted on either side of the Atlantic and not to be committed totally to the US circuit. (He was to win this battle and with it a freedom for all other Europeans as well.)

At times too, the intricate politics of the game seemed to obscure the playing of it and yet Seve knew that his place in the history of the sport would depend solely on the number of major titles he had collected by the end of his career and not the number of ripples or rules changes he had made during his time.

What was needed was some clear unequivocal act that would lift him out of the pack and place him without question among the great players and in so doing end all this speculation and argument about his worth and his place in the history of the game.

Augusta had to be the place and the Masters itself the occasion for this demonstration. The first time he saw Augusta with its rolling terrain and towering trees, he felt a oneness with it.

It was a feeling that, no matter how many Masters he played for the rest of his life, the enduring rival would always be Augusta itself. It was a battle between the two of them. If Seve lost this rather private duel then somebody else got the prize of the green jacket, but he never doubted that Augusta National was his principal foe.

His emotions were difficult to define. At first there was affection because its tree-lined fairways and terrain reminded him of Royal Pedrena where he had learned golf and where the game itself had taken on a meaning it would never lose.

That in itself meant that he played with a style that had been fashioned to cope with such terrain; he shaped shots through the air to find their target. That was the first lesson of golf he had learned as a boy.

But there was more to it; when he was locked in combat with Augusta, there were moments when he seemed to reel under the shock and crises the great course threw towards him but, like a fearless heavyweight caught napping by a counterpunch, he would simply shake his head clear and get back into the fray.

Nearly every hole at Augusta had its own story to tell of these furious skirmishes with Seve; of miracle escapes or ruinous disasters. There was the fifth hole where in 1980 he had hooked so badly he had left the ridge of the fairway and the ball had plunged halfway down the hill of the next hole in among the shrubs and the trees with no sight, no hint of the green's whereabouts.

But Seve had found a way – a sublime recovery that found its way through a tiny gap in the foliage then soared free to find the green. It had been the most staggering display of skill and daring and for years after people would take their friends to the spot from where Seve had performed the miracle.

There was another Ballesteros shrine on the seventeenth, although more precisely it was to the edge of the seventh green which flanks the left-hand fairway of this closing hole. Seve hooked there and was allowed a free drop.

The fans expected him to chip back to the fairway in the hope of getting down in a wedge and putt to save his par. He perceived another strategy and carted the ball high over the trees that seemed to have formed an impenetrable wall a few yards in front of him, imparting such force on the ball that it finished close to the flagstick and helped him to a birdie three.

These were the moments he savoured when it seemed quite clear that the most important talent of all was to keep a score going by whatever means and not necessarily to produce a flawless textbook display of middle-of-the-fairway consistency.

Anyway it gave the lie to those rivals who regarded him as a lucky player; he had recovered too often and from too many outrageous places for that sort of success to be a matter of sheer good fortune.

Perhaps the most difficult aspect of the day-to-day routine of tournament golf is the need to maintain some continuity of play and flow despite the intervals between one round and the next – those hours spent between an early finish one day and a late start in the following round.

That week at Augusta had been more difficult than usual because the fierce storms had not only caused delays but had forced officials to cancel Friday's play because the greens and some fairways were flooded. It was a day of frustration for Seve who had finished one stroke behind the lead on the opening round and sensed he had struck a rich seam of form that could be good enough for him to run away with this title – provided the magical touch did not fade. That, too, was the reason for his impatience.

By the time he had begun to play at the end of the field for the second round, it was obvious he might not complete eighteen holes before darkness fell that day. Even so, in the gathering gloom he had been absolutely right about his form and snapped up three successive birdies before being told to stop play on the eighteenth tee and return the following morning to finish off.

Not once during all these preoccupying diversions did he lose sight or sense of what seemed an impending showdown with the best performers in American golf who had assembled to contest the title. It was a feeling of destiny; a sense of a moment that had been preordained and

Seve and Augusta were old foes who had each scored victories over the other in various encounters. His most crushing failure was to come in 1986 when his chances submerged in the lake on the long fifteenth hole. *Phil Sheldon*

could not be avoided.

Even the third round, which was to leave him one stroke behind the lead, served simply as a prelude to that moment. Thus on the final day he presented himself on the first tee knowing the complete outline of his awesome task.

He had to engage in his customary duel with Augusta, its subtleties, snares and towering scale and at the same time thwart – or at least contain – the collective talents of Craig Stadler, Tom Watson and Raymond Floyd, if he was to prevail. Yet he knew that if he could defeat Augusta itself then the others would have no hope against him.

He was paired with Watson and at 1.25 p.m. precisely launched his assault with a savage drive over the right-hand bunker across the valley and beyond the hill on the other side. It was to be the warning shot to one of the most remarkable salvos of scoring in the championship history.

In a curious way too, he was about to engage his other two rivals, Floyd and Stadler, who were following him, in a long-range piece of psychological warfare because he knew they could see every move that he made.

He punched a seven iron approach into the green and minutes later the roar of the crowd told the two trailing professionals the news they did not want to hear as Seve earned his birdie and was now tied with them for the lead.

Watson, at his side, gave no hint of his feelings. He would not concentrate on the man but focused instead on the course itself. He had told himself that if he could

play the first nine holes in 34 – two under par – he would not be far away from the lead because the pressures of the final day – the closeness of the title and the stifling awareness that one slight mistake could lose it for ever – were enough to deter the kind of uninhibited behaviour of earlier rounds, when there was still time to redeem mistakes, and that knowledge encouraged a freedom of strategy. On the last day, there are no more chances and even the bravest man plays tightly. That at least was the common notion.

But what happened next seemed to suggest that Seve had suddenly decided to leave them all behind: to kill their spirits with a rapid burst like a marathon runner who breaks early and hopes the margin is wide enough – and his stamina strong enough – to keep the rest at bay until it is over.

In truth, that kind of decision can never be a conscious one; never part of a deliberately timed or orchestrated plan, because not even the greatest striker knows what is about to happen to the ball as he stands over it in preparation for his swing. All that Seve could bring to the moment was his prodigious talent, his experience, an overpowering urge to win that went beyond mere hope, and the inspiring effect on him of this course, this event and these rivals. For him, there was some point to all of this that went beyond the demonstration of athletic excellence. But then there always was.

He coiled himself into a fierce drive through the avenue of trees along the second fairway and down the other side of the hill so that the ball finished 300 yards from the tee and there were still 255 yards to find the green.

Seve reached for his four wood knowing that all the risk would be in the last few yards of the ball's journey and even then only if he struck it absolutely correctly because in its dying moments as it came back to earth, it still needed sufficient power and height to carry the bunker guarding the green and roll on towards the flag in the right-hand corner.

The noise of the impact was as sharp as a rifle shot and echoed round the trees so that those who stood there knew it had been perfectly struck. Then they looked quickly to catch its flight and those who missed just stared at the green waiting for a sign. And suddenly there it was, a little white speck a few feet from the flag.

Watson watched impassively, his face drawn tightly, jaw set firmly and eyes narrowed. Such a blow might have devastated lesser men or at least conveyed that awful sense of doom that this was not going to be their day. But Watson had been in too many tight corners, seen titles won and lost in the bizarrest fashions, ever to give up hope.

His own stroke sent that message clearly enough to Seve because his ball followed a similar route towards the green and was so perfectly aimed that the crowd began to roar in anticipation as it rolled on line towards the hole, clipped the rim and rolled on to finish beyond Seve's ball.

For one exhilarating moment it had looked as though one stroke of genius was about to be capped by one of even greater quality. If nothing else it showed Seve the level at which he would have to perform if he aspired to win.

He waited impatiently while Watson lined up his putt for a possible eagle and as the ball stopped inches away and the American tapped in for the birdie, he was already making his own preparations. This time there was to be no mistake and the ball flopped into the hole for an eagle three. Seve was in the lead.

But, more than this, he was chasing a score; an incredible tactic on a day when good sense cried out for safe play. On the next hole the ball finished close but the putt for birdie edged away at the last moment. Yet, there was clear evidence how this round was to be played: Seve was not about to back off from Augusta.

His next stroke put that conclusion beyond doubt. He stood on the fourth tee and gazed at the green more than 200 yards away on the other side of the valley and above that area of trees the professionals jokingly call the 'Delta Reservation Desk' because once in there, the recovery takes so many strokes the inevitable result is an early flight home.

He selected a two iron and drilled the ball towards the target and saw it stop just a few inches from the hole. The birdie putt was a formality. He had played the first four holes in four under par and he had left his close rivals gasping to keep up.

A quick look at the leaderboard told him that he had virtually shaken off Stadler and Floyd but he knew Watson, though trailing, would not give in quite so meekly. The two of them were locked in a man-to-man conflict in which they could focus on each other's play and at

The pattern of succession. Just as Watson had toppled Nicklaus to dominate the game, now he had become the target for Ballesteros. And by the time they reached Augusta's short twelfth on the final day in 1983, Watson sensed the change-over was complete.
*Phil Sheldon*

times draw inspiration from it.

They came to the long eighth hole which climbs the hill through the trees and turns when it reaches the brow, so that the green is blind for the long second shot needed to reach it. Watson was four strokes behind and knew he had to narrow that gap before they came to the awesome homeward nine holes where even the fearless Seve might find trouble.

Watson needed to get home with his second shot to a green he could not see. He stood in the middle of the fairway, reached for his driver, aimed on a line where he suspected the green would be and picked the ball cleanly from the mown grass. He could only wait to hear from the crowd whether it had worked and he was not disappointed. The ball finished 25 feet away and he holed the putt for an eagle three.

In that moment he had cut Seve's lead to two strokes and struck a crucial tactical blow. More than that, it had become a test of wills between these two powerful men: it was Seve's 'destino' against Watson's indomitable determination.

And it was to reach its climax on the next green when Seve hit an approach close enough for a realistic chance of a birdie. Watson could not afford to let him break away again so he too went for his birdie putt, but the ball sped 4 feet past. Seve holed. Watson missed and collected a bogey five.

The irony of it all was that Watson had covered those nine holes in the thirty-four strokes he had thought would be good enough, but instead found himself four strokes behind the leader. Perhaps both

sensed that it was the end of his challenge and that Seve had seen him off.

But now there was nobody on whom to focus; just a vague threat of names from the leaderboard. That was how it had been in 1980 when he had been ten strokes clear on the final day and started to squander them until mercifully he ran out of holes before he could make more mistakes and won by four strokes.

Now it seemed to be happening again. His long approach to the tenth green caught the bunker and cost him a bogey five. He over-hit his tee shot on the short twelfth to the back of the green to drop another stroke.

In the crowd, his father watched anxiously as the boy grappled with these threats to his own fate. What it needed now was much more than skill. It required almost raw courage not simply to play the strokes – any one of which could ruin him – but to restore control over his own morale and purpose.

On the treacherous thirteenth hole round the left-hand corner of the forest, he was in the trees. It was as though he was beckoning the rivals he had left far behind to come and catch him up again.

And if they saw from the leaderboard that he was in serious trouble they might just do it. Clearly, he could not afford to give more hope because to lose now would be to lose twice, having seen them all off in that devastating burst at the start of the round.

This was no time for miracles but instead he needed sound play and common sense. Accordingly, he jabbed the ball back to the fairway, lobbed an approach over the creek to the green and took two putts for his par.

The crisis had passed. The remaining holes became a march of honour as he scored the most important triumph of his life. It had been three victories in one. He had conquered Augusta. He had vanquished the best American golfers. And he had triumphed over his own fears and mercurial temperament.

And when it was over, Big Baldomero held court with the press. He told them he had made the journey this time because he knew Seve would win. They smiled. But, some sensed that he had witnessed again the embodiment of all those heroic qualities he too had discovered within himself all those years ago when he rowed the village boat across Santander Bay. He could die a happy man.

# CHAPTER FOUR

# John Mahaffey and the life that almost got away

Even when all the pieces of his life were put together again, there was still no precise reason why the nightmare had happened and John Mahaffey saw no cause to probe. It was best forgotten and not spoken of again.

In any case, it would have been too easy to explain the entire episode as simply fitting the clichéd case history of a young man of talent failing to live up to his own great expectations and then being so totally overwhelmed by the agonies of defeat, that life itself sinks into one long unconditional surrender.

And yet the obvious ingredients for such personal disaster were probably always there. He was a Texan, a brilliantly successful amateur golfer and in possession of an intellectual ability that had earned him a good degree in psychology.

When he became national collegiate champion, there were those who sensed they had seen the first signs of the rightful successor to the mighty Jack Nicklaus and, truly, that this young man had all the qualities of greatness.

He had impressed even the great Ben Hogan himself, who not only invited him to play golf, but subsequently ensured that when he turned professional John Drayton Mahaffey had a comfortable contract with the Hogan company.

A man of Hogan's judgement, who was not only revered as the finest striker in the world but was notorious for his reluctance to offer any praise to other players, could hardly be wrong. And when his golfing wisdom was handed down in such a personal manner to Mahaffey the world could only wait to see what the young man would deliver.

That may have been the start of the problems – this promise of so much to come. Those early years on the professional circuit were rewarded with encouraging and measured success and seemed totally in proportion to the progress of a talented novice learning his craft slowly but thoroughly.

He was no giant. His strength would always have to depend on accuracy and judgement. Where the supermen could launch the golf ball huge distances from the tee and allow themselves the forgiving luxury of short irons into the green, Mahaffey always knew he would

Mahaffey epitomized the game in its traditional form. Intelligence, skill and strategy made him a refreshing hero. But the pressure of great expectations became too much. *Peter Dazeley* trail far behind and have to rely on the longer clubs to find the targets.

Not a strain of course, even if it was an enforced style of play rather outmoded by the modern game. Mahaffey could cope with it and clearly underlined that fact when he won the Sahara Invitational at Las Vegas in only his second full season as a professional.

Here truly was the high flyer who could dominate the next age of tournament golf. In those early years, once he had found his winning stride, his prize earnings rarely dipped below $100,000 a season. Moreover, he was ascending the money list with every year that passed, and had rapidly reached that special point where it was expected he would soon win one of the world's four major titles to confirm his obvious class.

Maybe all the troubles could be traced to that first big chance he fumbled, because it meant he faced the added burden of having to atone for the failure to prove he was not stifled by the task of winning. Right on cue, he produced the best score on the 1975 US Open at Medinah in Chicago – his fifth year as a professional – only to find that somebody else had done it too. In the play-off he had lost to Lou Graham.

It had been a disappointment of course but Mahaffey had seen it coming that day in the eighteen-hole play-off: his putting was out of touch and he knew he could not cope with any sustained challenge from Graham. But these were early days and there had to be other chances.

True enough, a year later he had arrived in Atlanta for the US Open and on the third day had so dominated the contest and his rivals that he held a six-stroke lead as he stood over a shortish putt to go seven ahead. He missed, and it all started to get away from him.

He had refused to play safe on this fearsome course and had aimed myopically at every flagstick no matter what perils surrounded it. Yet such bravado endures only as long as the confidence remains – like the tightrope artist who must not think how far it is to fall. And when Mahaffey missed that putt he was somehow aware again of his own fallibility and it showed.

And yet, even though his lead was to all but vanish, there was still a consuming belief that on the final day this really would be his championship because of the manner in which he had controlled it. In fact the varying margin of his lead would matter little to the overall inevitability of the outcome – just as the fisherman plays the line in-and-out never doubting the catch will be landed.

But this particular script had a different ending and afterwards Mahaffey could only console himself with the memory that he was beaten by one of the most brilliant match-winning strokes in the history of the sport and one that would be immortalized in the record books in the manner of those famous decisive shots by Gene Sarazen at Augusta, Bobby Jones at Royal Lytham and St Annes and Arnold Palmer at Royal Birkdale. But even that thought was not enough to ease the damage and pain he had suffered. Of course there would be more chances but even he had asked plaintively, 'I can't keep losing

It was the scale of his failures in the big championships that began to fill Mahaffey with self-doubt and made him wonder if he could ever win in the best company. *Peter Dazeley*

# COURSE CARD

| Hole | Yards | Par | Hole | Yards | Par |
|------|-------|-----|------|-------|-----|
| No 1 | 469 yds | 4 | No 10 | 462 yds | 4 |
| No 2 | 343 yds | 4 | No 11 | 371 yds | 4 |
| No 3 | 425 yds | 4 | No 12 | 603 yds | 5 |
| No 4 | 549 yds | 5 | No 13 | 185 yds | 3 |
| No 5 | 379 yds | 4 | No 14 | 360 yds | 4 |
| No 6 | 195 yds | 3 | No 15 | 453 yds | 4 |
| No 7 | 395 yds | 4 | No 16 | 230 yds | 3 |
| No 8 | 244 yds | 3 | No 17 | 322 yds | 4 |
| No 9 | 480 yds | 5 | No 18 | 456 yds | 4 |
| Out | 3,479 | 36 | In | 3,442 | 35 |

**Total 6,921 yards par 71**

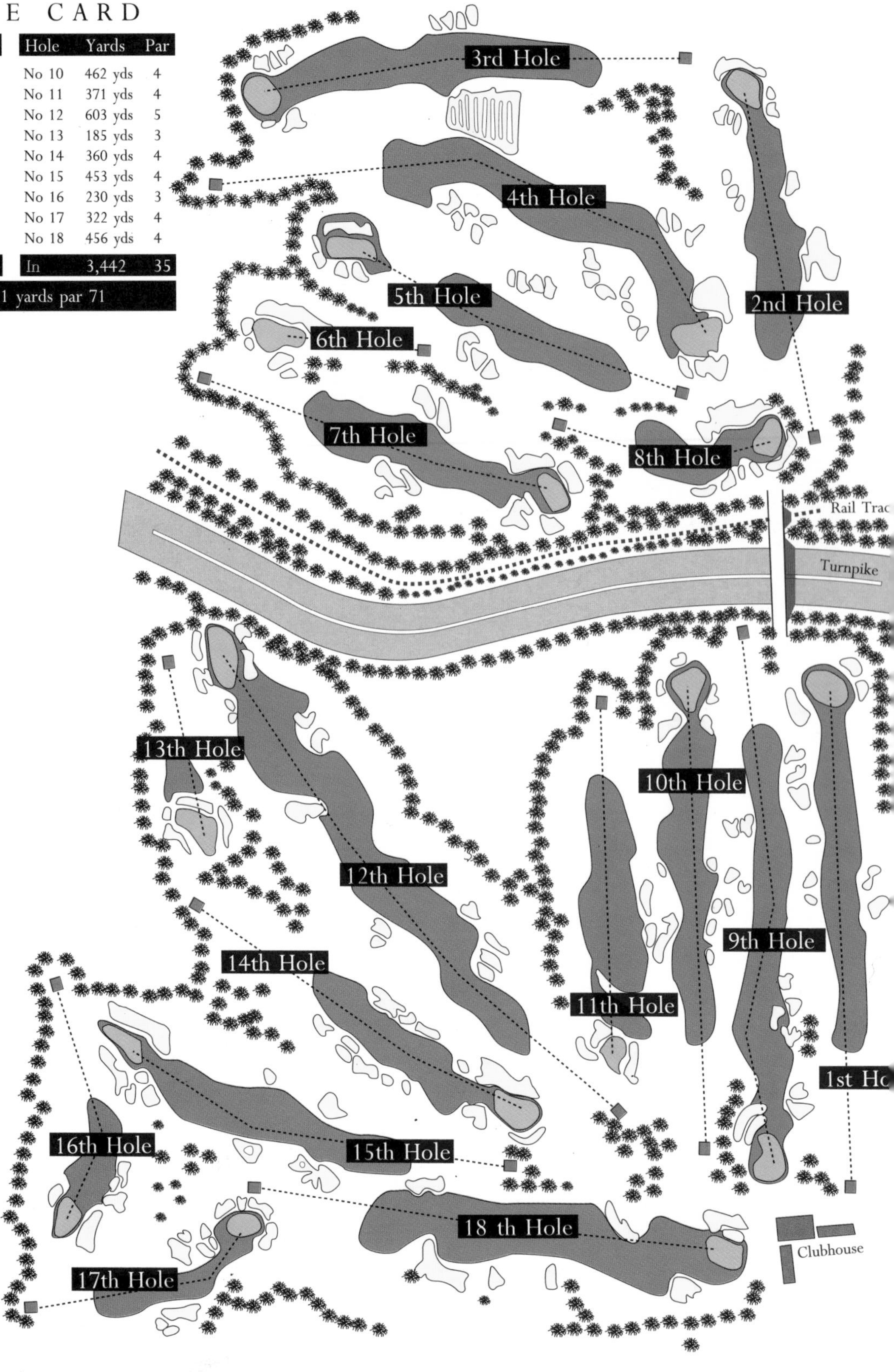

Oakmount

3rd Hole

2nd Hole

4th Hole

5th Hole

6th Hole

7th Hole

8th Hole

Rail Trac

Turnpike

13th Hole

10th Hole

12th Hole

9th Hole

14th Hole

11th Hole

1st Hc

16th Hole

15th Hole

18 th Hole

17th Hole

Clubhouse

And suddenly the prize belonged to him. And Mahaffey had earned his place in history as the 1978 US PGA champion. Nobody could ever take that away from him. © *PGA*

this tournament, can I?'

He had stood in the rough on the last hole trying to cope with the awful realization that he was not strong enough to thrash the ball free from the long grass and up and over the lake in front of the green. The ball was buried too deeply so he faced the agonizing dilemma of knowing he required a stroke of enormous power to overcome the perils but sensing, even as he stood to the ball, that he could not play it. It was doomed to failure.

The bermuda grass tangled with the clubhead and he knew as the ball lurched into the air that it would not reach the green on the other side of the water. He could only watch with mounting anguish as it plummeted into the depths so heavily that the widening ripples marked another wasted chance – and then were gone.

If only the memory of that failure had disappeared as quickly and easily. But there was more of this painful ritual to be endured and Mahaffey could only watch as his playing partner and chief rival, Jerry Pate, a newcomer in his first year as a professional, fearlessly drilled a five iron from the same rough to the green for a spectacular and historic win. In modern times only Jack Nicklaus had won a major title in his first professional season.

In that single stroke, Pate had demonstrated the brazen confidence of a young man who does not know how difficult the game can be. But more than this, he had not been damaged by experience because in truth such memories of what-might-have-been serve only to bear witness to what can, and will, go wrong.

Mahaffey could only stand and watch all of this. If the world is divided into winners and losers, he had still not solved the mystery of the difference. And even before they reached the green Mahaffey knew in which category he and Pate were to be found on that particular day. He walked over, shook his hand and declared quietly, 'Nice shot.' It was an admission of defeat.

Afterwards, in the months that followed, when word got out about his heavy drinking and the break-up of his marriage, the sages of the locker-room concluded that this was the true price of those defeats and the hurtful cost of failing his own high expectations of himself.

It was never that simple. There is an unblinkered honesty with which a golfer views himself, that makes him fully aware of his personal weaknesses and flaws no matter what he admits to the outside world. It is the basis of all confidence and self-esteem which in turn produces that essential ability to trust oneself under pressure. A man is ill-equipped without such knowledge and he knows it.

To the outside world, this was a heavy fall from grace that might end only in oblivion. The divorce, when it came, took a hefty settlement based on his big earning years. But now he had lost the knack of playing Mahaffey-style and within a year the high earner had grossed less than $10,000 prize money.

His friends on tour knew of his turmoil and consequently endured and forgave his behaviour, which at times could become tiresome and rather boorish. There were other problems too. He had injured his left elbow yet played on through the pain without treatment and not knowing the severity of the condition.

But there glows within every professional golfer the small flame of inextinguishable optimism; a belief that the next hole, the next round, the next tournament will change everything for the better. Even when a player is on the threshold of despair with his form, there is no thought of respite because next week, miraculously and without warning, it could all change. The game is littered with tales of such overnight transformations and that thought alone keeps all the struggling pros trying against the odds.

Perhaps the odds were too high because Mahaffey's run of misfortune took another wrong turn. No sooner had the elbow started to mend under treatment than he fell off a ladder and broke a bone in his right hand. If it had not been so cruel, it would have been laughable. But the sum total of all his bad luck prompted the general but unspoken belief that Mahaffey was no longer a force within the game. The great hope had faded without trace and with so much promise unfulfilled.

It was also a self-defeating predicament in which his life lacked purpose because he was confronted by evidence of his own failings and his inability to overcome them. And yet there had to be more. There had to be a way back. When he met Susie and she became his wife, the first steps of the comeback had been taken.

He mattered once again. He was important to someone else. And in that awareness, the self-esteem that had made Mahaffey such an exciting prospect in his sport began to reawaken. Susie, for all her affection, could see the stark reality of the choice that faced Mahaffey.

She told him bluntly, 'You can wish for success but unless you knuckle down and really work, you will never get it.' The message was clear enough. Mahaffey had swathed himself in thoughts of what should have been. He felt sorry for himself but here was Susie telling him that his future – their future – both on and off the fairways, lay in his own hands. It was his choice.

He was to reflect afterwards: 'It really hit home. I really was feeling sorry for myself. Susie helped pick me up. She inspired me to go out and do something. That's when I started working harder and practising.'

When he arrived at Oakmont in Pennsylvania for the American PGA championship of 1978, his fellow professionals regarded his appearance as part of the rehabilitation process. He did not bother with drink and the physical injuries had healed. Even so, there was nothing to suggest that he could be considered as a contender.

The top of that particular bill was being shared by Tom Watson, the new hero, and – of all people – Jerry Pate, who had dealt him such a heavy blow at Atlanta two years earlier. They were all happy enough to see their old friend back on the scene and even delighted that he was keeping pace, albeit a few safe steps

He needed, at times, to play to his physical limits to keep within reach of the powerful young challengers who had brought new values to the game. Mahaffey knew, therefore, the margin between success and failure was dangerously narrow. *Phil Sheldon*

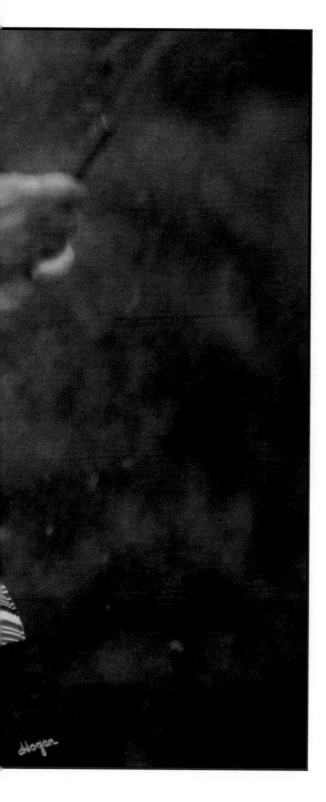

behind them, in the chase for the title.

And yet at the start of that grey, humid final day at Oakmont, the best Mahaffey seemed able to expect was a finishing place high enough to give him the confidence to carry on in competitive golf. He was seven strokes behind Tom Watson who was leading and showed no sign of releasing his grip on the occasion.

While some of Mahaffey's fellow professionals may have been aware that he had toiled for hours on the practice ground to regain his swing and to overcome the trauma of flinching when he hit the ball in case his hand and elbow jarred, they could not have known how the sum total of his experience had made him a stronger man.

The swing was the same but he felt spiritually stronger and fiercely determined to make up for lost time and wasted chances. So it was that he found himself teamed with Watson and Tom Weiskopf in the last group of the day. Just ahead of them, Jerry Pate was in another threesome so that all were well aware of every move that was to be made on that momentous afternoon.

Mahaffey could see almost from the start that Watson was not producing the kind of flawless golf that had taken him into the lead. Worse still for Watson, the fearless putting touch had gone. He began to make mistakes and could not retrieve them with a redemptive putt. He bogeyed the sixth and seventh holes and was falling back into the pack.

Watson's dilemma seemed to lift Mahaffey's spirits, because his aim was perfect to most greens and the putter was relentless in his hands. By the time he ran down a massive birdie putt from 35 feet on the sixth and another from close range on the eighth, the gap between them narrowed incredibly to three strokes.

The excitement intensified as the audacious prospect of a Mahaffey victory began to take obvious shape. But Watson had other ideas as he drilled a four wood into the heart of the ninth green then holed to putt for an eagle. It was not the first time in Mahaffey's career that a wonder stroke had threatened to crush his hopes.

Yet this time it would be different because there was more time and not the last-minute finality of that devastating stroke with which Pate had taken the US Open title from him in Atlanta. He was five strokes behind but there were still enough holes left to change the outcome this time – weren't there?

Watson proved that truth on the next hole. He drove perfectly but the ball finished in a divot mark. He jabbed the second shot free but never had quite enough control and had to play his third from a greenside bunker. He came out poorly and three-putted.

Mahaffey seized his chance and with an outrageous putt from 45 feet wiped away three strokes on one hole to be only two behind again. Yet neither of them could forget about Pate in the match ahead. He still lurked and was still lethal.

Mahaffey was now totally inspired. On the next green he ran down another putt from 25 feet for a birdie to push his score to seven under par and moved only one stroke behind Watson. Pate was still

hovering one stroke back yet Mahaffey, with an inexplicable conviction, suddenly sensed he had a chance.

By the time they reached the thirteenth they knew from the scoreboard that Pate had birdied the hole. Watson missed the green to drop a stroke and suddenly all three men were tied for the lead. It was now abundantly clear to all of them that this title could hang by one stroke – good or bad – over the closing stretch.

In such moments, the identity of an opponent blurs. His reputation and achievements diminish and he becomes simply an obstacle to success. Moreover, Mahaffey was transformed from the sad onlooker he had been for almost two seasons. On the fourteenth green, he stroked home a putt from 4 feet and became the outright leader of the championship for the first time.

But he was not on his own for long and the memories of Atlanta came back to haunt him as he played the fearsome sixteenth hole. He had left his tee shot a long way from the hole and, suddenly, was obsessed with the thought that he was not going to give this one away through errors as he had done in that US Open.

The sad result of such dithering and distraction was a long putt that finished too wide of the mark to make sure the second would drop and, ironically, he had made the mistake he had tried to guard against and was back eight under par with Pate. The only consolation was that Watson had also slipped back a stroke. Now it was between Mahaffey and Pate – and not for the first time.

It was then that the scoreboard showed

the sickening news. Ahead of them, Pate had pushed his score to nine under par and was playing the last hole. Worse still, Watson had come back to eight under par so that as they followed on down the last hole, both would need a birdie to tie unless Pate faltered.

The groans from the crowd surrounding the final green told them that Pate had missed his chance. His approach finished on the edge of the green and his first putt halted 4 feet from the hole. When he struck the putt, he thought he had read the line perfectly but the ball stayed out. He had bogeyed and was back to eight under.

A birdie from either Mahaffey or Watson would clinch it. But it was not to be. This dispute was to move into extra holes and Pate almost finished it there and then at the first play-off hole when his putt ran over the edge. But Watson chipped and putted to save himself and Mahaffey earned his par.

As they walked after their tee shots at the next hole Pate turned to Watson and said, 'John is going to birdie this hole. I know it.' Pate was in a poor lie in the rough and could not reach the green with his second shot – the exact role reversals of that US Open scenario two years earlier.

He was out of it and he knew it. Watson made the green, but was some distance away. Mahaffey, as predicted, was 12 feet from the hole. Watson missed. Mahaffey stood over his putt to become champion. He knew how much the ball would break over the surface because earlier that afternoon he had played from almost the same

spot – and missed.

This time there must be no mistake. This time he could only trust the hours of practice and hardship he had endured to bring him to this moment. This, after all, is what it had all been for. Now he must trust his judgement and his touch. In essence he was on his own.

There was too much to think about to even dwell on the enormity of the moment and suddenly the ball was in motion on its way and then it disappeared into the hole. Mahaffey dropped his club. His caddie hugged him and the comeback was complete. Moreover, neither of his beaten foes resented it. Pate could only reflect, 'No one really knows how much John deserved to win this one. When I won at Atlanta, John should really have won that Open.'

Now it was over. Mahaffey was at last the champion everybody always expected him to be. Simply, he had arrived a little behind schedule and he mused, 'I have paid my dues. There have been a lot of disappointments but they made me stronger. It was my turn.'

There was something else too; a truth that is perhaps the secret of all success at golf and suddenly it had been revealed to Mahaffey who understood at last: 'You can't make yourself win. You've got to let yourself win. That's what happened. I let myself win.'

And then there was the biggest triumph of all. What Mahaffey did that day was to show to millions of no-hopers, even beyond the realms of golf, who had reached the depths in their personal lives, that there is a way back.

# CHAPTER FIVE

# Nick Faldo and a place in history

He always woke early and this day was to be no different. No matter how it might affect the rest of his life or how he would be judged, it would have its beginnings in simple routine.

And yet for Faldo, the wait until the afternoon, before he would be summoned to the first tee of the Old Course, stretched before him like an eternity. Worse still, there was time to think, time to dwell; to ponder on the permutations and quirks of fate and fortune.

At such times it is the awareness of how destiny, particularly in this sport, hangs on the roll – perhaps a half turn – of a ball, that is most punishing of all, because no matter how flawless and machine-like the technique, these vagaries of luck still decide the outcome.

But there remained the eternal challenge of golf; all the planning, preparation, strategy and confidence can never promise anything more than the chance of a reasonable tilt at success. The result is never more than an ability to take that chance if it comes. There is no guarantee. That is its strength and its weakness but it remains enough to lure its devotees to play each day in hope.

In a curious way, Faldo's prodigious tally of personal achievements did not seem to help much, either, at this time, even though he was regarded by those around as virtually invincible. While the mood might not last, at the moment he could do very little wrong on the fairways.

He had captured the US Masters for the second time in the spring. That in itself had been a gigantic accomplishment, because not only had he equalled a rare performance from Jack Nicklaus by successfully defending his title, but he had also scored a last round 65 to confound all those whispers that suggested he was incapable of grabbing titles but could only plod along in the hope that somebody else might lose them.

That image had clung to him from the days of Muirfield when he had scored eighteen successive pars in the final round to become Open champion while the American, Paul Azinger, dropped strokes at the seventeenth and eighteenth holes to lose. It always seemed such a harsh attitude by his critics that the manner of his win mattered more than the achievement itself.

Playing par golf could never have

Norman saw that 1990 Open at St Andrews as a showdown and talked about it frankly. Faldo said nothing. He knew he had to defeat the entire field. *Phil Sheldon* been a deliberately safe strategy in the last round of a championship, if only because such caution was bound to come a cropper at some point and what Faldo's critics seemed to have missed or ignored was that he was putting for birdies most times during that round but missing, which is why he had to settle for par figures. It was simply a case of the putts not dropping, and not some stone-walling tactic calculated to grind down the opposition.

And yet, it was a style of play that seemed to fit the popular impression of him; or rather the view conveyed by the media. At the best of times there was a fragile truce existing between the writers and Faldo but this week at St Andrews the treaty had been torn up and he found himself involved in some tabloid newspaper sensationalism.

The story was in the papers before he knew about it. Some reporters had talked to the American professional, Scott Hoch, on the eve of the championship, and asked him about Faldo, who had beaten him a year earlier in the play-off for the US Masters. Hoch had missed a short putt for victory which seemed to have underlined Faldo's role as one of the game's slip-catchers as he emerged as champion.

It is unlikely that anybody, except Hoch himself, will ever know whether he thought he was being funny when he opened up to the pressmen about Faldo's apparent lack of popularity and how he had been less than generous with his comments in victory. It was all news to Faldo, yet it had been given point this week because they were to be paired together in the first two rounds of the Open at St Andrews.

The incident did nothing to allay Faldo's distrust of a media that seemed always to expect as much from him off the fairways as on them. There had been another controversial incident earlier in the year when he came home in triumph from Augusta and jokingly offered a television chat-show host his famous green jacket to wear.

The show was not even over before Augusta National Golf Club had been informed by a newspaperman and Faldo was censured in print for what he had considered nothing more than a joyful and harmless gesture.

It all added to the enormity of the task that now confronted him. He led the Open championship. But more than that, he led it by a hefty five-stroke margin. He had left all his rivals far behind. The best golfers in the world had struggled and failed to keep up with his superlative scoring rate over the Old Course.

And yet that was the frightening aspect of it all. To lose now would be a disaster which everyone would seize as a sign that perhaps after all he did not have the calibre of a true champion. Moreover, he would be assailed by his own doubts too if this one slipped away from him.

But then Faldo knew that any victory depended as much on what other people did as on his own performance and that this would be the great imponderable that would tease him throughout that final day.

He had endured his share of cruel defeats in his time, some of which had even questioned his nerve under the pressure of the big moment. There had been a US Masters title which slipped away in the final round, as well as a World Matchplay battle in which his boyhood rival Sandy Lyle had fought back from the brink of defeat to beat him.

That evening Faldo and his first wife, Melanie, had gone back to their rented house in silence and simply packed their bags and left for home. There was simply nothing to be said about such a savage reversal of fate. And yet the experience had simply confirmed his growing conviction that his golf swing would not hold up under pressure and unless he learned a new technique in which all the body parts worked to order, he would spend the rest of his days getting close to big titles but never quite able to bear down and take them.

There had always been this clear-eyed realism about him; a brutal honesty that at times made his own life and the lives of those around him rather difficult especially when he was struggling to break through. There was a fierce streak of self-reliance too; he was never a team man but always a solo performer. He had spurned the school football team and the role as goalkeeper to take up competitive swimming at which he had excelled and he spent time living rough in the Scottish Highlands as part of an Outward Bound training course. Faldo had a self-possession beyond his years and a firm idea of what was best for him and his career.

On such terms, two years earlier, he had astounded the world of golf, and particularly his fans, by deciding at the end of 1984 to risk all chance of success while he went away and learned how to play golf again. More specifically he wanted to build a new golf swing; one that was more functional and reliable than the willowy flourish with which he had grown up to become one of the best players in Europe.

He knew the risks and that to relinquish his customary role as a leading contender whenever he played while he mastered a new technique might rob him of a competitive sharpness that would never return. It was after all an unspoken fear of most great players that the touch – the talent – might suddenly desert them overnight and without reason.

The game has been littered with such sad and frightening cases of professionals who suddenly discovered without warning or reason that they could no longer play as well as they knew they were able. There was no obvious reason and therefore no cure and they were never the same again. Faldo was deliberately putting himself in that situation yet he was spurred on by an impatience with his own limitations. He could see the difference between himself and the players of true class and there was no satisfaction in remaining second-best for the rest of his life.

On reflection, the great transformation might never have occurred had he not met David Leadbetter, a former touring professional whose own playing achievements were modest to the point of obscu-

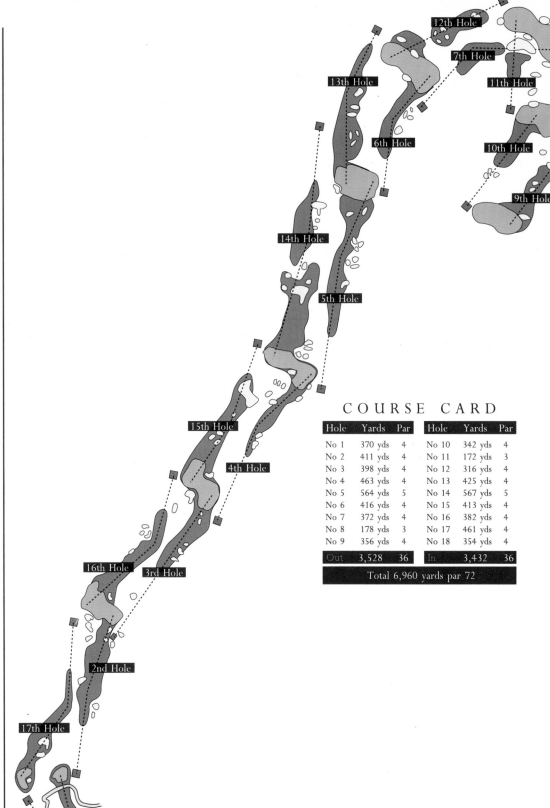

# St Andrews

**12th Hole**

**7th Hole**

**13th Hole**

**11th Hole**

**8th**

**6th Hole**

**10th Hole**

**14th Hole**

**9th Hole**

**5th Hole**

**15th Hole**

**4th Hole**

**16th Hole**

**3rd Hole**

**2nd Hole**

**17th Hole**

**1st Hole**

**Clubhouse**

**18th Hole**

## COURSE CARD

| Hole | Yards | Par | Hole | Yards | Par |
|------|-------|-----|-------|-------|-----|
| No 1 | 370 yds | 4 | No 10 | 342 yds | 4 |
| No 2 | 411 yds | 4 | No 11 | 172 yds | 3 |
| No 3 | 398 yds | 4 | No 12 | 316 yds | 4 |
| No 4 | 463 yds | 4 | No 13 | 425 yds | 4 |
| No 5 | 564 yds | 5 | No 14 | 567 yds | 5 |
| No 6 | 416 yds | 4 | No 15 | 413 yds | 4 |
| No 7 | 372 yds | 4 | No 16 | 382 yds | 4 |
| No 8 | 178 yds | 3 | No 17 | 461 yds | 4 |
| No 9 | 356 yds | 4 | No 18 | 354 yds | 4 |
| Out | 3,528 | 36 | In | 3,432 | 36 |
| Total 6,960 yards par 72 | | | | | |

Faldo brought a measure of aloof concentration not seen in the game since the great days of Ben Hogan. For him it was a job of work at which the public were allowed to look over his shoulder. *Phil Sheldon*

rity, but who had made an exhaustive study of the game's technique and formulated his own conclusions on the best method by which to gain the high level of consistency needed by competitors when they were under stress.

His words made sense to Faldo, yet Leadbetter warned him that there could be no half-measures if he wanted to learn the method. He had to commit himself totally to getting it right even though that meant enduring the frustration of setbacks that assail all learners plus, in his case, the public curiosity and criticism about what had gone wrong with his talent. He would also have to come to terms with his lowly position down among the supporting acts in almost every tournament, while people he knew he could beat were taking the prizes.

The learning process would take at least two years because it had to be imposed on an old, almost instinctive method learned in boyhood and one which would keep breaking through in moments of stress, so that at times Faldo would find himself at odds with both techniques and not in control of either.

Essentially Faldo knew that his problem as a tall man was to get all the parts of his body, the angle of the arms, the position of hands and elbows, the set of the knees and the hips, in the correct spot every time from which to make a good swing at the ball. Leadbetter's method, in simple terms, was to allow the big muscles of the body – in the back, arms and legs – to dictate the pattern of the swing so that the linkage of all these

parts generated power and consistency.

And it had worked, although he had needed most of the two years to eliminate the looseness from his swing through a series of drills and exercises that he practised even before striking the ball during a tournament. He had re-emerged as a player who could stand up to the pressure and one whose method at last could match his enormous will-power and ambition to make him a winner of championships.

That should have been enough but he then realized that the cruel demands of fame extend to the manner of his victories, their locations, their circumstances and, most of all, the manner in which they were taken. The irony of it all was that his first two major victories had been diagnosed as the result of mistakes made by others although such a view ignored the fact that he had played well enough to find himself waiting to win.

By the time he had captured his second US Masters title, that hurtful perception that he won titles by the back door had been laid to rest. And now here at St Andrews, at the home of golf itself, he found himself with the chance to end that damaging opinion for ever.

There were other compelling reasons for an outstanding personal performance from Faldo that day, the most important of which was St Andrews itself and its spiritual significance. This was where the game began. It remained a shrine to which thousands of pilgrims flocked each year while millions more made their devotions to it through the observance of the rules of the game which is governed virtually worldwide from this grey-walled university town on the edge of St Andrews Bay.

St Andrews always bustles and in a noticeable way leads two separate lives, both of which exist comfortably and independently side-by-side, first, as the Mecca and most popular resort in the world for golf tourists and, second, as the seat of learning for hundreds of red-gowned students at one of the oldest universities of Europe.

Most of the shops, bars and hotels in the streets down towards the Old Course are given over to golf and golfers, but only a few hundred yards up the hill and in the centre of town, life goes on without any apparent awareness of the nearby shrine and those pilgrims.

The Old Course defined the character and nature of the game – particularly that axiom that insists it was never meant to be a fair one and that links golf, with its humps and hollows and consequent bad bounces and misfortunes, tests the man as much as his golf. Moreover 'the old lady', the name used by the locals, had been part of the game's most historic moments.

Here the legendary Bobby Jones acquired his first experience of golf in its original form, and was so exasperated that he tore up his scorecard in disgust during his round, because he could not understand the course's subtleties among the sandhills and pot bunkers of what seemed a featureless landscape.

But he was to learn that the art of golf lies in imaginative and disciplined play and it was in this form that St Andrews gave the game to the world and, no matter

how much it was altered around the world to suit conditions of terrain and climate, the philosophy would not change.

The procession of champions over its fairways bore testimony to its importance and the special demands of skill it required in finding a consistently safe route between its perils. How easy the courtly Tony Lema had made it all look in 1964 when he arrived late and put his complete faith in the local caddie, Tip Anderson, who steered him around the course to victory.

But there had been personal tragedy, too. Here, Doug Sanders had seen his dream end cruelly on the final green when he missed a short putt that would have made him Open champion in 1970 but instead allowed Jack Nicklaus to fight again in a play-off and win. Then, too, the mighty Seve Ballesteros had ended the American domination of golf and almost certainly the Tom Watson era with his inspired triumph in 1984 when the American was on the threshold of a hat-trick of titles.

There was a factor common to all these winners at St Andrews. And it was best summed up unwittingly by a man who had been one of the most important influences in Faldo's career and even after his death continued to exert respect and reverence for his acknowledged wisdom.

Gerald Micklem was an immensely rich man who devoted his life to golf, first as an amateur player of international distinction, then as an administrator and eventually as a benefactor and mentor to emerging young players of talent. One such was Nick Faldo, a teenager who had

The old Faldo swing in action during
the 1978 British Open at St Andrews
was too loose and willowy and
always likely to go wrong as he tried
to get his body parts in the right
position. *Phil Sheldon*

The new Faldo swing, thirteen years
later at the 1991 PGA championship
at Wentworth. The big muscles
have been developed to provide
more control of the linkage system
between arms, hands and club.
*Peter Dazeley*

no family pedigree in the game but had taken to it after watching a televised tournament and had demonstrated immediate skill.

Micklem loved St Andrews. He considered it to be a special place, not only in its beauty and history but in the philosophies the course observed. And he conveyed this love and respect to Faldo.

He once reflected, 'The enduring truth is that winning at St Andrews sets even the champions apart. It lifts the truly great golfers away from the rest. There are Opens. And then there are Opens at St Andrews. Therein lies the difference.'

That morning before the final round Faldo could reflect on a succession of battles already won that week, each of them crucial and decisive in their way and yet serving only to bring him to the point now where he had to fight again in the biggest battle of all.

In the press conference earlier that week he had confessed, 'I thrive on Majors. It is nerve-racking when you get into a position to win one. But you know that this is what it is all about. What all the hard work and practice has been for.'

The memory of what happened at Medinah in the US Open a few weeks earlier served to confirm that truth. And yet as the putt he needed on the last green of that Chicago course halted inches from the hole denying him a place in the play-off, he not only knew the minimal margins between success and failure but also resolved, 'Right, now for St Andrews.' It had been a declaration of intent and not a consoling thought. He

was determined to win and now he held the massive lead required to do it.

For a time that week it had seemed that Greg Norman had returned to take his revenge on the Open after the cruel misfortune of the previous year at Royal Troon when he had scored an astounding 64 in the last round for a place in the play-off and then lost to add another unwanted memory to his growing collection of near-misses.

This time he was back in force and had opened up with a 66 that included towering displays of powerful striking in which he actually drove the twelfth green while the group ahead were still putting and then he later hit his drive to the edge of the final green for his sixth birdie of the day. The game, it seemed, could not have been easier and Norman never more determined.

But Faldo was there just one stroke behind on 67 and in a way he had capped Norman's grandstand finish by holing a 40-yard pitch-and-run shot for an eagle two to earn the applause of a delighted crowd.

How ironic that this should happen there of all places on that green. The last memory of the eighteenth at St Andrews had been a sour one when he refused to play on in the gathering evening mist during the Dunhill Cup against Des Smyth and, in protest, angry students had hung banners from the windows of the red-bricked Hamilton Hall across the road from the last green when he returned the next morning – and lost.

By the end of the Open's second round, the inevitable showdown had materialized between Faldo and Norman, both tied on 132. The Australian, in what was probably unwitting war talk, declared, 'I am playing well and putting well. When I get the ball on the green, I feel I am going to make the putt. As for a shoot-out with Faldo, it doesn't matter who I play.'

But it did, although Faldo himself had wisely decided not to comment on the clash in view of the newspaper stories that had already assailed him that week. There would be enough to write about anyway at the end of the day without hyping this into a heavyweight contest and losing sight of the ultimate goal.

In truth, Faldo was conerned only with his game and score and not obsessed with beating his Australian playing partner on the day. But once they began, it did not take long for him to realize that Norman had lost all his confidence especially on the greens and was heading for a score that would quickly remove him from this contest.

And yet it could not simply be the pressure of the moment that caused this surprising decline – certainly not on the third day of a championship, even though it is the stage when contenders make their move and the shape of contest is invariably set. Perhaps there was some fundamental flaw which had triggered all Greg's disasters and which he would have to discover so that his achievements could match his obvious talents.

But Norman had gone and was just a memory. Now Faldo must protect his five-stroke lead to become champion. Before his tee-off time, he had spent an hour with Leadbetter but their session had more to do with boosting his morale than making any last-minute adjustments. And now it was time to start.

He took a two iron from the tee to deliver the ball into that massive flat landscape that encompasses the first and eighteenth fairways and then he lazily lobbed a sand wedge over the burn so that the ball finished 4 feet from the hole. He sank the putt and was six strokes clear.

He looked anxiously at the scoreboard to see if anyone was making a challenge as he found himself falling into a familiar pattern of playing par golf. Then the alarm bell sounded. Payne Stewart, the American PGA champion, had erupted into life and was closing the gap between them.

He had birdied the fifth and sixth holes and whenever Faldo glanced at a scoreboard there was more depressing news of the American star's charge. By the tenth he was only three behind and as he stepped from the twelfth green, having holed a 7-footer for a birdie, he was only two strokes adrift from Faldo.

Faldo was now engaged in an even greater battle with himself: to control his mind and nerve, if only to play the kind of golf he knew he could produce. His one hope was that Stewart, playing considerably ahead of him, would run out of holes before he could do much more damage in terms of birdies and that he might even make a few errors. Either way, Faldo would have a few holes in hand to know what was required of himself.

It was a curious feeling and one that he had experienced before whenever he was involved in the pressures and travails of winning. It was a sense of being another person; of standing outside himself looking on at all the actions and decisions. The body itself seemed to send its own message that all was well and that it could handle all the strains.

Then Faldo saw the message for which he had been waiting. Stewart had begun to falter. He dropped a stroke on the thirteenth hole and began to fade so quickly that he dropped shots on the last two holes. By the time Faldo had run home a birdie putt on the fifteenth, he was four strokes clear and knew he needed to play wisely and sensibly over what remained of the Old Course to win.

He would take no chances with the treacherous seventeenth – the Road Hole where so many hopes and scores have been ruined. His tee shot took the line off the wall and out into the fairway and he knew he would play for a deliberate bogey by finding the front edge of the green with his approach.

That gave him a long putt across and up the slope which he thought would almost certainly take him three putts to hole out. Within minutes he had earned his expected bogey five and walked a few paces to the final tee. The spectacle was breathtaking.

The grandstands behind the green were full and hundreds of fans lined the street that flanks the right-hand side of the last fairway. There were faces peering from every window in the street and from Hamilton Hall too. It was an unbelievable moment, as though Faldo was playing golf into the very centre of the town.

At that moment Faldo held the complete and undivided attention of the entire world of golf as millions of global viewers witnessed the crowning moment by satellite television. He was the focal point of that universe as he launched his tee shot safely away from dangers of the road on the right-hand side and began his march to a place in sporting history. What remained of this championship was merely a formality.

The statistics of his triumph were impressive but somehow mattered less than the lifetime of effort and sacrifice – not always just his own – it had required to bring him to this point where he had taken the irrevocable step of joining the truly great players who measure their lives by the Majors they have amassed. His life would never be the same again because he would always have the evidence that he was rightfully in that special company which stands above all the rest.

It was a moment to be shared of course and the most important people in his life took their places alongside him by the final green to acknowledge the cheers. There was his second wife, Gill, who had sustained and supported him through the depressing days of toil on his new golf swing, and had endured without complaint the enforced solitude as he spent hours and hours on the practice ground. Perhaps nobody would ever know, not even Faldo, the degree of effort involved in maintaining a balanced home with their children while he went through the self-inflicted trauma of learning to play golf again.

There, too, was Fanny, his Swedish

caddy, who had actually taken lessons from Leadbetter so that she could understand the component parts of the Faldo swing and be able to spot impending errors as he competed on the fairways. She had also played her part in lifting his spirits in moments of extreme pressure.

And then there was the army of fans who now roared their appreciation of his ability and achievement. He had been a professional almost sixteen years and at last he had won them over. It was the greatest victory of all. Faldo had become their hero. Not just their champion. It was a new beginning for them all.

# CHAPTER SIX

# Gary Player and just a little help

On this, of all nights, he could be excused from his punishing fitness ritual. But the temptation did not linger and, while the others in the house slept, Player began lifting his weights long into the night.

But then it wasn't simply the quest for fitness that drove him through this inflexible daily routine, although such value was self-evident and had been manifestly obvious that day at Augusta. Rather, it was the discipline such strain and effort imposed when, even in reluctant moments, he felt compelled to be in complete control of his own pysche so that sometimes it was difficult to determine whether the recurring prospect of hoisting those weights was more bleak than the actual process itself.

Some might say there was a mystical quality to it all; and perhaps the daily campaign of self-improvement, the onslaught against his own imperfections might well have its origins in the same compulsion that had prompted ascetics to spend their lives in the conquest of self. In a sense, the path to success in golf – perhaps in other pursuits too – begins with the elimination of error. This, in itself, demands clear-eyed, self-examination and recognition of such flaws.

And, in a way, golf paralleled Player's philosophy of life in that both were constant and relentless tests of character, choice, judgement, discipline and all the other aspects that go to complete the human jigsaw. He had learned from childhood the hard realities of life and in particular the mental need for self-reliance and the personal toughness to sustain it. He had been eight years old when his mother died.

His father worked down the gold mines outside Johannesburg. His elder brother, Ian, was fighting the war in Italy. His sister was away. Thus Player was obliged to structure his own young life on strict lines even if there were times in the evening when he was too frightened of the dark to enter his empty home but would wait in a nearby bus shelter for his father to return. In time, he had conquered that fear and, though he was too young to recognize the process as such, had learned the strength of will-power and the manner in which it can overcome problems and change fortunes.

His success story had a familiarity

The old master and the young apprentice who shared his jubilation that day at Augusta in 1978. The venerable Player taught Seve the most important lesson of all. Never write him off. *Phil Sheldon*

The sand traps held no terrors for Player. He had lifted bunker play to an art form through hours of practice and coped confidently on his way to victory at Augusta in 1978 when the pundits were looking elsewhere for a winner.
*Bob Thomas*

about it; a diminutive man who felt the need to assert himself in a world of giants and who therefore tried harder and worked longer to achieve that goal. Indeed the only reason he ever began his weight-training programme was to become strong enough to hit the golf ball as far and as straight as Arnold Palmer, Jack Nicklaus and the other American heroes he knew he must conquer.

It was simply part of the improvement process. Even in his early days when he came to Britain with such an unorthodox swing that one senior professional had advised him to go back home to South Africa and try and find a safe well-paid job as a club professional, he knew how huge the task of building a sound technique would be.

He sought out the great specialists – the bunker players, the putters, the mid-iron players – on the practice ground and studied their techniques for as long as they hit shots. Then he would work tirelessly in an attempt to copy what he had seen.

He knew there was an essential need to become a superlative bunker player, if only to have the freedom to attack the flagstick invariably protected by sand traps, so that he could still redeem himself from the sand if he made the slightest error. Accordingly, he worked tirelessly learning to become the best bunker player in the world.

More than this, he saw golf as an athletic pursuit; or rather, he did not follow the fashionable view that the best exercise for golf was the golf swing itself and there was no need for any disciplined keep-fit routines to improve general strength and well-being.

When he had embarked on his fitness programme, he had been regarded as a crank by his fellow professionals. They scoffed at his penchant for peanuts and bananas to give himself energy. They were amused at his insistence on sleeping on the floor of hotel bedrooms, and in aeroplanes, for that matter, to protect his back.

What made them rather uneasy was his unashamed references to the Almighty as though golf was a lofty mission and he had struck some pact by which he would be rewarded for leading the good and clean life. He was a zealous man who was so open and honest that others sought to find the flaw.

He was so positive that he talked constantly in superlatives, at times reaching the threshold of nonsense when praising one Scottish golf course for having the finest flagsticks he had ever seen.

Yet the importance of his attitude was that he never felt defeated by the prospect of a difficult test but sustained his determination by the thought that somebody always won the top prize at the end of the week and it might as well be him provided he remained in a positive mood.

He knew early on that his life could never have been just a simple matter of sporting achievement. He came from South Africa and he was its most recognizable citizen; certainly the best-known South African to travel the world and in consequence he became the easy target for anti-apartheid activists.

# A ROUND TO REMEMBER

Even in his greatest moments, Player was never far away from crisis or drama which seemed essential ingredients for his style of play. He was no stranger to the rough either - as he showed in the 1961 British Open at Royal Birkdale.
*Sidney Harris/Phil Sheldon*

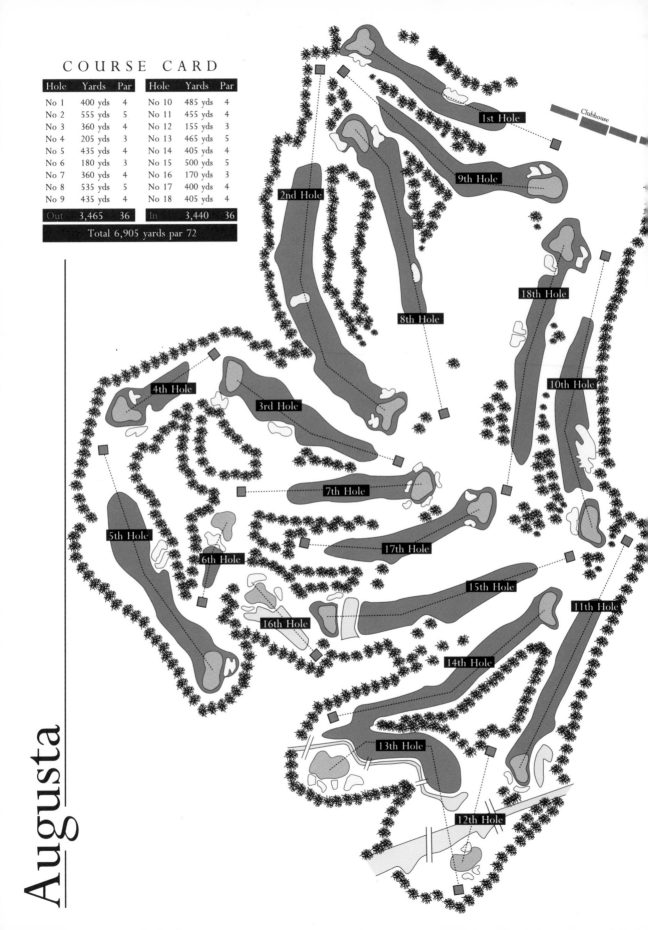

# COURSE CARD

| Hole | Yards | Par | Hole | Yards | Par |
|------|-------|-----|------|-------|-----|
| No 1 | 400 yds | 4 | No 10 | 485 yds | 4 |
| No 2 | 555 yds | 5 | No 11 | 455 yds | 4 |
| No 3 | 360 yds | 4 | No 12 | 155 yds | 3 |
| No 4 | 205 yds | 3 | No 13 | 465 yds | 5 |
| No 5 | 435 yds | 4 | No 14 | 405 yds | 4 |
| No 6 | 180 yds | 3 | No 15 | 500 yds | 5 |
| No 7 | 360 yds | 4 | No 16 | 170 yds | 3 |
| No 8 | 535 yds | 5 | No 17 | 400 yds | 4 |
| No 9 | 435 yds | 4 | No 18 | 405 yds | 4 |
| Out | 3,465 | 36 | In | 3,440 | 36 |
| Total 6,905 yards par 72 | | | | | |

Clubhouse

1st Hole

9th Hole

2nd Hole

8th Hole

18th Hole

10th Hole

4th Hole

3rd Hole

7th Hole

5th Hole

6th Hole

17th Hole

15th Hole

16th Hole

11th Hole

14th Hole

13th Hole

12th Hole

Augusta

He had not helped himself, of course, by insisting in his early years of fame that he supported the apartheid system and was quick to point out that it was no different in concept from the manner in which the Americans had confined the Red Indians to their so-called reservations.

He had believed that a separate-but-equal system would work until he realized there was to be no equality and during the process of this personal change he was to become the target of apartheid demonstrators, particularly in the United States and Australia, to a point where his life was threatened.

In 1969, he had been attacked by spectators during the American PGA championship in Dayton, Ohio, when ice cubes, programmes and golf balls were thrown at him and he played the last round surrounded by an armed guard.

In the 1971 US Open championship at Merion, he was given another armed police guard in the house where he stayed while police cars also patrolled the street all night. In Australia he also needed an armed escort for protection.

Throughout it all he refused to quit; refused even to take the easy option that was available to him of quitting South Africa and bringing his family to the wealth and prosperity that was waiting for him in the United States.

He simply refused to let the protestors win. He was not ashamed of South Africa. He loved its rugged and raw beauty. He loved all its people. He could be reduced to tears of unexplained joy as he beheld the wilderness of the Karoo desert.

If his life truly was a mission, then these threats formed part of the inevitable test and he would prevail against them with the help of the Almighty. In the cold hard real world, there might seem no place for such blind faith yet Player's belief was unshakeable.

In any case, he was always bemused and slightly indignant that no other notable sportsman had been called to answer for his country's controversial policies in such a manner, particularly Arnold Palmer or Jack Nicklaus, even though the United States had been engaged in a variety of controversial ventures from Vietnam to Cambodia.

The problem was that Player simply could not be ignored. His phenomenal success on the fairways made him a high profile personality. He had won all the four major championships of the world and previously only Jack Nicklaus, Ben Hogan and Gene Sarazen had ever managed that achievement in the history of the modern game.

He had won the British Open three times; had captured the US Open once and taken the US PGA championship twice. By 1978 he had two American Masters to his credit. His place in history was secure. And as he turned up at Augusta that week for the 1978 Masters, it seemed there was not much else than a place in history to think about. He had turned forty. He had not won an American tournament for almost four years. A new generation of heroes had emerged and the Era of the Big Three – Palmer, Player and Nicklaus – had almost certainly had its day.

# A ROUND TO REMEMBER

He was the first golfer to treat golf as an athletic pursuit. He trained for it, observed special diets and kept himself in peak physical fitness. It was to be the secret of his lengthy career and one of the reasons why he won the gruelling World Matchplay championship a record five times. *Colorsport*

There was not much left for Player to do but make the occasional nostalgic appearance on the great occasion at which he would always be welcome and spend the rest of his time looking after his hugely successful horse-breeding business in South Africa.

His love of horses had stemmed from his boyhood when a friend had taken him to a farm outside Johannesburg for the weekend. With his first pay cheque earned as an assistant to Jock Verwey, the club pro whose daughter Vivienne he would later marry, Player bought a share of a horse.

By the time he had made his initial fortune from golf in the early 1960s he had bought himself a stud farm and in the fullness of time he would move to a bigger complex in the great horse-breeding region of the Karoo in Cape Province and became a noted and highly successful owner quite apart from his reputation as a breeder.

And yet, at heart, Player was simply a golfer. All he wanted to do was play the game he had learned as a boy. Everything else was a bonus – some of it engrossing but still secondary to what he enjoyed most: the pursuit of a golf ball under his own skill across country. His business managers could look after his fortune. He would stick to what he knew best.

But the prospect of decline was becoming apparent; or rather this awareness that he might not be able to answer the demands of golf at the very highest level or withstand the strains and pressures of being closely involved in the battle for all four rounds.

There was a time when he had revelled in the pressures; when such drama brought out his strengths. He had played an astounding shot over trees and across a lake to secure victory in the 1972 US PGA championship at Oaklands Hills. He had drilled a fairway wood to a faraway green he could not see to set up his 1968 British Open win at Carnoustie over Jack Nicklaus. He had played back-handed from the side of the clubhouse with his putter to win the 1974 British title at Royal Lytham and St Annes.

Every Player victory seemed to be characterized by some moment of crisis from which a match-winning stroke was produced, because nothing less would do. Even his first Open win at Muirfield in 1959 held its own drama as he thought he had thrown the title away by taking six on the last hole and had to wait most of the afternoon before he realized nobody had caught him.

Then, too, his first Masters win at Augusta in 1961 had been bizzare because he was sitting in the clubhouse when he became champion while Arnold Palmer, from the middle of the final fairway, took six to throw it away.

They had been the great days and what made them so special was the sense of involvement, win or lose, that came with being one of the best players in the world and pitted against the other great performers. They were all great friends but on the fairways their sole purpose, as Player has declared, was to beat each other's brains out.

Perhaps those days were gone for ever.

Where was the evidence to the contrary? The new hero, Tom Watson, was setting fresh and exciting standards and a new breed of rivals – Johnny Miller and Lanny Wadkins among them – were in close pursuit. It was the dawn of a New Age and, it seemed, no place for the likes of Player so that maybe graceful retirement was the answer.

But within Player, there still burned the conviction that he was not finished and that given the right circumstances there might still be one last great major title waiting for him. There was, after all, no appropriate moment ever to give up, not even when good sense insisted there was nothing else to do.

That much he had proved back in 1965 when he had come back from the dead against the American Tony Lema after being five down with nine to play in the World Matchplay championship at Wentworth. It had been such an inspired revival that Player had collapsed to the ground after he won in extra time, while Lema, until his dying day a year later in a plane crash, had often woken up in the night wondering how and why it all went wrong.

No, Player would never give up and could never admit he was finished. He had brought a smile to some PGA officials when he declared he would change his schedule if he won the Masters that week. And when he told a close friend on the eve of the final round at Augusta, that he could still win if he scored a 65, there was no more than unconvinced, but loyal agreement.

How could it be otherwise? He was

The ferocity of Player's swing sometimes left him off balance at the completion. But he was strong enough to make solid impact with the ball when it mattered. *Phil Sheldon*

seven strokes behind the leader, Hubert Green. He was at least ten years older than all the leading contenders and there was nothing to suggest he had seized upon any rich vein of form to change his fortunes. In any case Tom Watson, who was closely pursuing the leader along with Rod Funseth, had been winning tournaments all season and expected to do so again.

How and why Player thought about that special prayer as he walked to the first tee, he could never recall: 'I can do all things through Jesus Christ which strengthen me.' He had said it often during those depressing days in America and Australia when he attempted to play competitive golf while being attacked by apartheid protestors.

And yet the words came back to him and filled him with extraordinary strength as he met his playing partner, a young Spaniard called Severiano Ballesteros, on the first tee. Seve had been depressed that he was seven strokes behind the leader and in his own words had left things 'too late'.

Seve was about to learn a lesson that would transform the rest of his life and ensure that he never ever gave in to feelings of defeat before the last putt had dropped. It is a style that has characterized his play ever since.

In strict terms they were a warm-up act, playing perhaps forty minutes or at least three holes ahead of the main stars who seemed destined to contest this title on the final afternoon.

And, true enough, both Player and Ballesteros plodded in workmanlike fashion through the opening holes not causing much interest as they went. Not even when Player birdied the ninth hole to edge his overall score to five under par did there seem any need for the fans to take much notice.

As he walked across in front of the clubhouse to the tenth tee, Player was still five strokes behind Hubert Green and three adrift of both Watson and Funseth, so that perhaps the best he could expect by the end of the afternoon was some polite applause for a tidy performance and decent score as an old timer.

'I can do all things . . . ' He lined up the putt from 25 feet and suddenly it was not a question of getting the ball close enough to make sure he holed the next one for his par. This one would drop. Player was six under par . . . and had begun to stir.

What transpired in the next two hours was the most extraordinary long-range encounter between Player and his rivals, which he turned into the stuff of match-play. Every cheer and roar from the crowd that greeted his masterful play worked as a weapon against his rivals to let them know they were under siege.

He snapped up a birdie on the short twelfth across Rae's Creek. Then he clipped another stroke from par as he rounded the left-hand dog-leg of the long thirteenth. He was now eight under par and the cheers exploded and echoed round the towering pine trees on that treacherous stretch of the course at the bottom of the hill called Amen Corner where so many scores and dreams have been shattered.

Green may have heard the cheers through the trees from the nearby fourteenth hole which signalled yet another Player approach shot within a few feet of the flagstick for another birdie chance. Green appeared unnerved and dumped his approach into the water in front of the green to drop a stroke. He was nine under par. Watson and Player were at eight under.

What remained of this championship was to take on the chaos and clamour of a bar-room brawl in which each man kept battling, not quite knowing what was going on, but convinced he must not stop trying until the dust has settled and, when it was all over, they could find the winner.

As Watson was marched down the thirteenth in pursuit of a perfect drive, he heard the roars from the fifteenth fairway. Player was unstoppable. He had just scored another birdie and was nine under par and tied for the lead with Green and Funseth.

The warning spurred the American into action. He drilled his long approach across the creek to the green, then rammed home a 20-footer for an eagle three. With that defiant stroke Watson swept past them all to take the outright lead.

Player's problem was that he was running out of holes while Watson had them in hand and could play accordingly. After all, the closing holes at Augusta can be savage and should never really be attacked – certainly not in the last minutes of the championship.

But is it not possible to do all things?

And in any case, what is there to lose if it fails? This is a title that must be won actively and not stalked defensively in hopes that others fail.

Accordingly Player hammered his tee shot over the lake within 15 feet of the sixteenth flagstick, and sank the putt for a birdie two. The roars and the scoreboards told Watson he had been joined in the lead at ten under par by the diminutive South African.

But Green and Funseth were still dangerous and refused to go away. Both earned their birdies on the long thirteenth which meant all four contenders were now ten under par. And what remained would determine which of them had the will-power and crushing determination to prevail against the rest.

Watson faltered first. He was desperate to break the deadlock and went for his birdie on the fourteenth green even though the better move would have been to settle for par. The ball lipped out and ran almost 3 feet past. Then, inexplicably, he missed the return putt to take a bogey five and slip back to nine under par.

In a moment he was joined by Funseth, a journeyman professional who seemed caught up and totally inspired by a level of drama that he had not previously experienced. Yet Watson had no intention of meekly surrendering to fate and instead hit over the lake on the long fifteenth, then left his putt close enough for a tap-in birdie to rejoin Green and Player in the lead.

If ever there was a time for blind faith in destiny and a solid golf swing, then this was it for all of them. All the hours of arduous practice, all those previous dramas they had all experienced, the wins and the losses, now had to somehow combine into an abiding strength which they needed as never before.

By the time Watson was sizing up his tee shot on the short sixteenth, Player stood over his own putt of 15 feet for his last chance of a birdie. As it dropped Player punched the air in delight. He had played the last nine holes of Augusta, by common consent one of the most difficult stretches in the entire world of golf, in thirty strokes. He had taken 64.

Truly he had done all things. His young partner Ballesteros – the one who had been on the same score at the start of the round and thought any challenge was too late – had tears in his eyes as he hugged the great man. He knew he had been a privileged witness to one of the great and historic performances in modern golf. And he would never forget any of it.

It had been a magnificent masterpiece of determined and courageous play. But was it good enough? Now Player could only wait and see how the others still on the course would fare.

It was to be an agonizing vigil. First, Green tapped in on the long fifteenth for a birdie. He was eleven under par. And Watson ran down his own putt on the sixteenth green for a birdie also to go eleven under par. Could either of them find the extra birdie to edge past Player and rob him of his third title and one that most observers thought he was well past winning?

The news that Player had already gone to eleven under par did not reach the scoreboards by the time Watson and Green assumed they had tied each other for the lead. But when it did, the effect was staggering. Green three putted the sixteenth to fall out of the lead. Then Watson came to the last and played a poor tee shot which caused him to struggle all the way to the green and left him facing a putt from 12 feet to save his par and tie with Player. For most of its journey, the putt looked as though it had been read perfectly but in its last moments, it failed to turn towards the hole and stayed out. Watson had missed and would have to settle for second place.

Now it was Green's turn as he came to the last green having struck a superb approach shot less than 3 feet from the hole. He was unquestionably one of the best putters in the world and he needed this stroke for a birdie that would earn him a place in a play-off with Player.

As he stepped over the ball, he heard the muffled voice of a nearby radio reporter. He stepped away, then tried again, but the putt was poorly struck and his moment gone. The ball had been sent on the wrong line and at the wrong pace to ever drop.

Player was champion. Truly he had done all things. As the press assembled afterwards, one cynical journalist remarked, 'I wonder what Gary's secret will be this time. Raisins? Peanuts? Bananas? Maybe God?'

He was not far from the truth though he did not know it. Player told them all about the prayer he had uttered throughout the final day and because he was the winner they had to listen. He saw no need to be bashful about it. It had been a good day's work for Gary – and the Almighty.

If faith can move mountains, it can certainly pick off the occasional major golf title. But, more than this, Player had offered example and hope to others – in all walks of life – who felt they were past it and written off. The battle cry throughout Player's life from the boyhood days in South Africa, through the traumas of those US demonstrations and serious illness had always been, 'Don't write me off!' It remains the most important prayer of all because it contains both faith and hope.

When all the celebrations were over and history had been made, Player went back to his weight-training ritual. Nothing had changed. A little earlier, Hubert Green went alone to Augusta's last green and tried that putt again. He missed. Nothing had changed there either.

# CHAPTER SEVEN

# Curtis Strange and the absent friend

He blinked back his tears but it was no use. Then he realized she was sobbing. It was her grief too. Both man and wife were shattered as they drove home because their dream had suddenly gone wrong and they could not understand it. This was not supposed to happen. This kind of failure had never seemed possible on the promised road to glory that Curtis Strange had always assumed lay ahead of him. This sort of thing happened to others. Not him. He had been touched by destiny.

It should have been the gentle start to the great adventure through life for Sarah and himself; the moment when they would take off to face the world together, knowing that his talent and their love for each other was all they needed to conquer whatever confronted them.

Yet, he had succumbed to the first test. And badly too. He had not even proved he was good enough to become a touring professional. The boy who had promised so much as an amateur, who had been noticed by the venerable Arnold Palmer and even awarded the great man's scholarship at Wake Forest University, had flopped.

It wasn't a matter of ability. That had been proven so many many times in the realms of top-class amateur play. He had been the national hero of college golf even winning the American title for his college and the individual title for himself by scoring a famous eagle three on the last hole when nothing else would do. Nearly every major amateur trophy in the United States had his named engraved on it. Nobody ever doubted that this young man was marked for greatness.

More than a rare ability that needed to be fulfilled, there was also a burning desire – a compulsion – to succeed that would never let Strange rest easy. It was more than a mission in his life. It had become a debt of honour, perhaps also a retaliation for the cruel blow fate had struck him in those boyhood years.

In those days, he had loved to be at his father's side. He would go with him just after dawn to open up the pro shop and clubhouse of the course he had just bought and stay there until business was finished for the day. He loved the bustle and business of golf-club life.

He loved, too, the solitary challenge of

Strange was to learn that talent is only part of the formula for success. By the time he reached the US Open at Brookline in 1988, he had acquired the resolution and courage to become the champion. *Phil Sheldon*

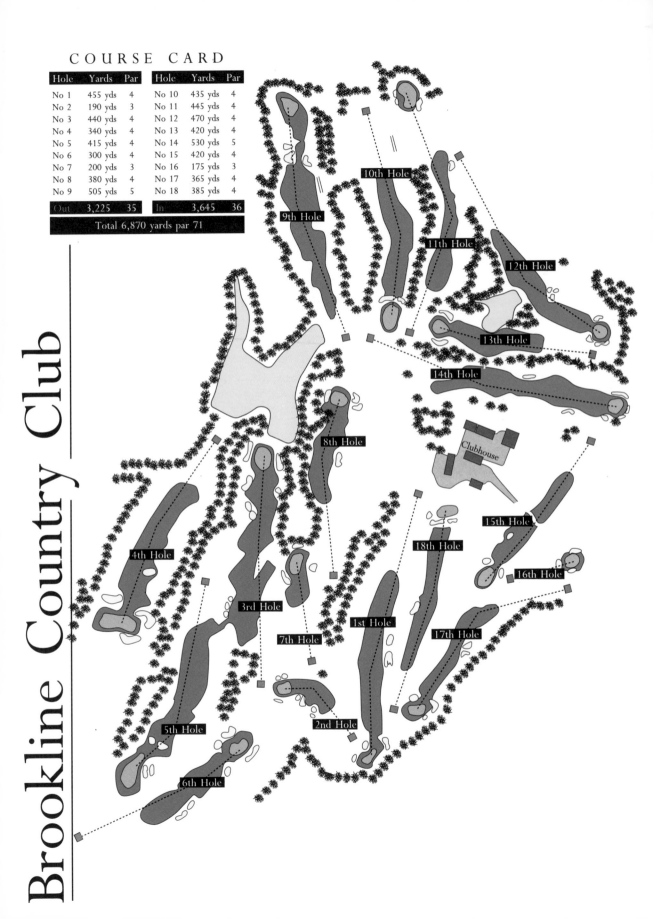

# Brookline Country Club

## COURSE CARD

| Hole | Yards | Par | Hole | Yards | Par |
|------|-------|-----|------|-------|-----|
| No 1 | 455 yds | 4 | No 10 | 435 yds | 4 |
| No 2 | 190 yds | 3 | No 11 | 445 yds | 4 |
| No 3 | 440 yds | 4 | No 12 | 470 yds | 4 |
| No 4 | 340 yds | 4 | No 13 | 420 yds | 4 |
| No 5 | 415 yds | 4 | No 14 | 530 yds | 5 |
| No 6 | 300 yds | 4 | No 15 | 420 yds | 4 |
| No 7 | 200 yds | 3 | No 16 | 175 yds | 3 |
| No 8 | 380 yds | 4 | No 17 | 365 yds | 4 |
| No 9 | 505 yds | 5 | No 18 | 385 yds | 4 |
| Out | 3,225 | 35 | In | 3,645 | 36 |

Total 6,870 yards par 71

9th Hole

10th Hole

11th Hole

12th Hole

13th Hole

14th Hole

8th Hole

Clubhouse

15th Hole

4th Hole

18th Hole

16th Hole

3rd Hole

7th Hole

1st Hole

17th Hole

5th Hole

2nd Hole

6th Hole

golf. He would spend hours on the practice range remembering what his father had taught him and slowly imposing it on his technique. It was curious that his identical twin brother Alan was not attracted quite so profoundly by the demands of the game but preferred the more stirring atmosphere of team sports.

There is within every son a constant ambition to earn the admiration of his father; a compulsion to shine and succeed so that the old man will smile, perhaps nod in acknowledgement that the lad is at last a man and has surpassed even his own achievements and aspirations.

Strange knew precisely where his field of endeavour would lie and where he would strike the closest rapport with his father. Tom Strange had been a distinguished amateur and friend of Arnold Palmer in their amateur days and, when both turned professional, Tom chose the club life and struggled to raise the cash to buy his own course in Virginia.

He was a sound judge of the game and passed on not only the basic principles of technique – the grip and the stance – that would never change throughout his son's life but he endowed, sometimes unwittingly, the philosophies and attitudes to the game that mark the difference between winning and losing.

He had told Curtis never to assume there was any task that was beyond him; no ambition that could not be fulfilled. And so the boy dreamed of the great moments . . . playing Arnold Palmer and Jack Nicklaus for the US Open and he has *this* putt to beat them all . . . and he makes it!

What wonderful dreams. It seemed those days would go on for ever. Then his father became unwell. Then seriously ill. No more visits to the golf club. The cosiness was about to go out of the young man's life. When his father died of cancer, Curtis was just fourteen.

Now there would never be a chance of showing his dad how good he could become; no chance ever to see that wide grin that seemed to split his face from ear to ear as Curtis held some great trophy aloft. He had gone away too soon; departed before the story started and there was nothing the lad could do to change things. It was, though he did not know it, another legacy that his father had passed on and one that was to serve Curtis through many crises in golf. Life – like the golf ball – has to be played as you find it and it is no use complaining that it should have been different.

The more immediate effect of Tom's death was that the family ran into financial problems. The golf course had to be sold and Nancy Strange had to go out to work to support her twin sons and young daughter. These were to be the hard times that served only to focus the young man's desire to become a success. It was a desire that went beyond the notion of playing supreme golf for its own sake – and beating Arnie and Jack in the process. That idea had been kid's stuff. This was the real world and Strange was painfully part of it.

He had inherited an impatience with his own imperfections. His temper would flare at times if things were not right for him. And now this high expectation of himself seemed to propel him at greater speed. A year after his father's death, he met an old family friend who was to take control of his life. Chandler Harper had been a PGA champion, and he not only made the young man a member of his golf club, but also began to tutor him.

Though Curtis could not realize it at the time, he was, piece-by-piece, becoming the product of the work and aspirations of wise men, each of whom would play a vital role in the building of a champion. The process had begun with his father. Then Chandler had taken up the cause.

Soon it was the role of Jesse Haddock, the slow-speaking, meticulous golf coach at Wake Forest University in North Carolina, which Arnold Palmer had attended and to which he had given a golf scholarship in memory of his fellow student and close friend, Buddy Worsham, who had been killed in a car accident. Only the best prospects were ever offered such a prestigious bursary. Lanny Wadkins, the PGA champion, and Jay Sigel, the great amateur champion, could bear testimony to that.

Coach Haddock knew he had a volatile player on his books. He even told Strange that he played his best when he was angry but that such fire must be used to improve performance and not overwhelm it. That much the young man seemed to have learned thoroughly as he collected whatever amateur honours came his way.

In the background, always at a discreet distance, lurked another figure who kept note of his progress. Nothing escaped the attention of Arnold Palmer who saw himself as a father-figure to the young protégé. The day after Curtis had married his college sweetheart, Sarah, they had stayed with Arnie and Winnie at the start of their honeymoon. What better beginning for the great adventure as husband and wife set off for a life in professional golf.

And now it had stopped. He had flunked the qualifying school tournament. And what hurt was the manner of his failure, because it suggested for the first time in his life that he could not always summon the precise strokes exactly when he needed them. For a player who had never experienced such self-doubt, the effect was alarming.

He had three holes to play and needed only to negotiate them in par to make sure he qualified for the tournament season. Yet somehow he lost control of the plan and the strategy. He could not contain the damage and each hole had turned into a nightmarish bogey so that he missed the qualifying score by a stroke.

Was he really suited to competitive golf? The amateur game had been glory-or-nothing. But this was a tough hard school with bills to pay every week. Maybe he should look for some other career. Sarah and he discussed these and other notions when they reached home. And yet despite their desolation they knew how close he had come. He was really just the other side of the fence – too close to be considered an abject failure. He would wait and try again.

What happened was no more than a hiccup in his professional career which

This was a triumph that belonged to both of them because Sarah, his wife, had suffered the same setbacks and heartaches on the way to this US Open title that now belonged to Strange. *Phil Sheldon*

# A ROUND TO REMEMBER

Some bitter memories would never be forgotten. He had thrown away the 1985 US Masters that he sensed should have been his when he hit into Rae's Creek at the thirteenth hole in the final round. *Phil Sheldon*

would be long forgotten in the perspective of time and diminished by the success that must lay in wait for him. And yet . . . and yet . . . when he had needed the shots . . . they were not there.

To the outside world, Strange found his step at the next qualifying school and began a methodical but inevitable progress towards the upper ranks of the tournament performers, so that with each season that passed he gained experience and self-assurance and in his third year had won a professional event. The wise men in the background took note. Everything was going according to plan.

He was still hot-headed of course, yet this was interpreted as encouraging evidence of the passion he summoned to his golf and his desire to succeed. As such, it could be tolerated in a world that was looking for new American heroes to succeed Arnie Palmer, Jack Nicklaus and Lee Trevino.

And yet, in his haste for success, he could sometimes overstep the mark. Quite surprisingly, he caused outrage and indignation when he verbally attacked a woman volunteer for distracting him as he played in the Bay Hill Classic in Florida. It was the wrong action in the wrong place because the event was run by Arnold Palmer who also owned the course. He was angered by the young man's behaviour.

Strange knew that not only had he offended the most important figure in golf and one who had looked after his interests but he had also behaved boorishly and let himself down. It took him two weeks to face the great man and declare, 'Mr Palmer, I lost my cool. It won't happen again.' Arnie accepted the apology without reservation.

His temperament began to come under a different pressure. His collection of week-to-week tournaments increased. His prize earnings rarely dipped below $200,000 a year and he was regarded as one of the most consistent commercial players in American golf. In one season he had even earned more than $250,000 without even winning a tournament.

But could he win a major title? He had progressed to that rare company of players for whom the next move must be the capture of one of the four major championships of the world if for no other reason than to underline their class. There have been numerous candidates who earned huge amounts of money but never collected a title and were therefore never accorded an enduring place in the history of the game.

Strange was too good for that. Everybody believed it to be true. And when he found himself four strokes ahead of the field with only nine holes to play in that extraordinary US Masters of 1985, they had assumed they were absolutely correct because he had played the most astounding golf to be there.

He should have been on the plane home after the first round. In fact he had booked a flight from Bush Field to Virginia for the next afternoon after he had opened with an 80 because he knew he was an absolute certainty to miss the halfway qualifying score. His caddie suspected that midway through that opening round Strange had given up, thrown in the towel.

By the end of the next day, the disillusioned caddie had been obliged to change his mind as he realized that he would be working throughout the weekend. Strange had undergone a remarkable transformation which began with a towering eagle three on Augusta's long second hole to start a barrage that would not finish until he had played himself back into the thick of the battle with a 65.

His old dad had been right after all. There was no task that was beyond him; no ambition too great to be fulfilled. And he had savaged Augusta with a vengeance, so that he stood on the threshold of the most outrageous victory in its history by giving the rest of this field of great golfers an extraordinary start in the first round on one of the toughest golf courses in the world and then catching them and romping past.

So it was, he came to Augusta's thirteenth hole and launched a perfect drive and saw the ball hit high on the curve of that fairway then settle down almost in the middle – but not quite. When he got there, he realized he was standing a little below the ball. No matter, a four wood would see him safely over Rae's Creek and on to the putting surface for a birdie or at worst a par five.

There were those who saw him take the wooden club from the bag and wanted to snatch it from his hand. He should have laid up and played short of the hazard. They argued he should have allowed the others to take risks to catch him. He could have lobbed the ball short then flipped it to the green for a possible one-putt birdie or at worst that par.

He was to say afterwards that it is not in his blood to back off. It never occurred to him to lay-up and play safe. What he needed was the right shot at the right time. But it was not there when he wanted it. The ball was always underpowered and though it did its best to reach the other side of the water, it hit the bank and toppled down to the edge.

Still not a problem. He could put on his waterproofs, stand on the water's edge and splash the ball to the green for a birdie or a par. It was not even worth taking a penalty drop. He swung and as the ball rose through the spray, it was evident it could not climb the bank but instead bounced, halted then rolled back to his feet.

Now the crisis had taken awesome shape. He tried again and though this time he was successful, there was never any real prospect of holing the putt. He had taken a bogey six and was in the process of handing this title away. Nor had the personal trauma ended because once again he had to reach for a stroke to guide him safely across the water in front of the green on the long fifteenth – and it was not there.

This time, the drive had been long and straight and he resolved that a four iron would deliver him safely to the target. But even as the ball became airborne, he knew it could not complete its proper journey and it plunged into the water. The young man was now in a daze. He dropped a new ball at the edge of the lake, pitched over too wide and needed two putts to hole out. He

# A ROUND TO REMEMBER

He told himself he had played this sort of bunker shot a thousand times before. It was easy and there would be no problems. Yet he needed it to save himself on the 72nd hole against Faldo and go on to win the Open in a play-off the next day. *Phil Sheldon*

had taken another bogey six and was out of the lead never to regain it. Afterwards he could only watch as Bernhard Langer donned the green jacket.

He was the man who had lost the Masters. His disasters formed the abiding memories of that championship as he struggled amongst the splash and spray vainly to retrieve his chances. Maybe he really was just a commercial player, good for earning money but incapable of finding those deep reserves of character and will-power that are needed to take command of the big occasions and make a true champion.

And yet what had Tom said all those years ago? There is no ambition that cannot be fulfilled. That must also mean that no failure – no matter how savage – carries an irrevocable sentence on a man's ability. Maybe his time would come. But how would he handle it? He knew he had allowed himself time during that final round to think about his dad and what tribute he would pay to him afterwards. Now the chance was no longer possible and in a curious way it caused him greater regret than actually losing the title.

Anyway, there was a living to be earned, a family to be supported, a trauma to be forgotten if possible. And sure enough the personal hurt began to ease with the years so that by the time he arrived at the Country Club in Brookline near Boston for the 1988 US Open championship his fortunes had been restored. He had earned more than three million dollars prize money in his short career. He had twice been top money winner and he had amassed an impressive array of com-

mercial titles. He was, everyone agreed, in commanding form as America's best player.

The wider historical significance of the occasion had not escaped him either because it was here at Brookline in 1913 that a young amateur, Francis Ouimet, who worked in a local sports store, had actually tied with Harry Vardon and Ted Ray in a play-off for the American Open title. Until then, the overseas stars who had given the game to the world had dominated the championship at will. And even the few American-based players who took the title were naturalized US citizens who had been born in Scotland or England.

Ouimet changed all that. He was American, born and bred, and he had beaten two of the greatest players in the world yet he never turned professional to enjoy the wider benefits of his fame. Curiously enough, American golf at Brookline some seventy-six years later was under siege again from the foreigners.

The European stars – Seve Ballesteros, Nick Faldo, Sandy Lyle, Bernhard Langer, Jose Maria Olazabal and Ian Woosnam – were running wild through international golf. They had won back the Ryder Cup after years in American possession and they were establishing a vice-like grip on the US Masters title at Augusta.

Clearly they had to be stopped. Strange was the man on form and thus the popular view in the press was that he was also the man most likely to do it. And he had obliged during the early rounds that week by keeping within reach of the leaders then edging past during the third round when decisive moves are generally made and the pattern of the championship is set.

With three holes to play that afternoon he was three strokes clear of his rivals. His swing was functioning fluently and obediently. He was repelling the invaders and setting himself for what could be a march of triumph on the final day. Or so it seemed. How ironic that crises so often grew from innocent, harmless and unguarded moments.

His approach shot to the sixteenth drifted fractionally off target and settled in a bunker to the right edge of the green. He came out to 8 feet but the putt stayed wide. He had lost a stroke but it was still not a disaster.

On the seventeenth he struck his approach safely to the green to a distance that should not have required more than two putts. But his first stroke ran too far past and he was astounded when the return putt spun round the rim of the hole and stayed out. Now he was only one ahead. Nor was his work yet complete because another approach found another bunker on the last green and he toiled from the sand to save par.

He had finished only one stroke ahead of Faldo and they would be paired together on the final day. The Englishman was still the reigning British Open champion following his 1987 Muirfield win and was now at the height of his powers, thinking only of acquiring major titles and in fact using week-to-week events to sharpen his game for those assaults.

The following afternoon, as they met on the first tee, there was no thought in Strange's mind that he was somehow playing for American pride and morale. He regarded himself and the rest merely as players and that their country of origin did not really matter. Yet he dismayed his more partisan fans by dropping two shots in the first three holes to allow Faldo to plod his way into the lead with par golf.

Strange could see from the scoreboard that the others had begun to fall away and this was to become a duel between Faldo and himself and that mercifully they could keep an eye on each other and manage their tactics accordingly. He had resolved not to think about his dad. He banished all memory because of what had happened at Augusta all those years ago when he got ahead of himself and never caught up.

Whatever this imminent triumph might mean personally or nationally or financially would have to wait until it was over. There was really no point in considering any of it until the last putt had been holed. He could see that Faldo was in a machine-like mood in which his swing relentlessly extracted par figures from every hole, so that when he himself birdied the seventh they were back on level terms as they headed towards the closing stretch.

Both were in a high state of tension as though afraid to take a decisive blow in case it failed and allowed the other man the simplest of victories as he capitalized on an error. But then Strange suddenly got his chance on the tenth hole for a birdie his rival could not match and moved a stroke clear.

But they were still both playing safe

Whether he liked it or not, Strange was regarded widely as the man to halt the growing march of European power in the game. Faldo himself typified this new fearless wave of international star who had turned up on American shores in the wake of Seve Ballesteros. *Karina Hoskyns/Phil Sheldon*

and edged cautiously to par fives on the long fourteenth. If Strange had thoughts of keeping his rival at bay, shot-for-shot, until they ran out of holes, he had to forget about it as Faldo snapped up a birdie on the fifteenth to draw level again. Now would they attack? Or would Strange once again be afflicted by the last-minute fickleness that had dogged him from the early days when he first tried to become a professional golfer?

Faldo squared up to his approach to the sixteenth green and cut the ball into a greenside bunker. Strange did not want to be short of the target and over-hit the ball to the back of the green into long grass. Faldo came out poorly some 20 feet past the hole and Strange could only jab his recovery to the edge of the putting surface. It looked like a pair of bogey fives until Strange quite suddenly ran down the putt for his four and Faldo missed.

It was a precious one stroke margin and it was all he needed to become champion but could he hold on to it? Would Faldo allow him to do so? On the seventeenth tee Strange reached for his three wood and delivered the ball into the middle of the fairway. Faldo went with his one iron and finished shorter, which meant he would have the first decisive strike to the green. The element of matchplay between them was now overpowering.

Faldo's approach did not scamper to the upper level of this two-tier green and he was a long way from the flagstick, which meant he faced a very demanding putt of both pace and line that had to be perfectly judged. Strange had to be on the top level with his approach and sure enough he lobbed the ball only 15 feet from the flag. Faldo would struggle to make his four. Strange had the golden chance of a birdie three.

The Englishman coolly judged it perfectly and left himself no more than tap-in for his par. Strange stood over his own putt that would give him a two-stroke lead. It was downhill and fast . . . be careful . . . let the ball trickle on line. As he touched it into life, he could see it was going to miss – just fractionally. But then to his horror the ball kept on rolling and rolling, stopping mercifully before it reached the slope to the lower level. Even so, he was 6 feet past the hole. And he was completely shocked.

It had not been a precise swing that he had needed this time. Just a putt to save himself and, once again, it had not been there. He missed the return. Faldo, grateful and surprised, was back on level terms. From the final tee Strange hooked his shot into the rough. He was clearly still dazed by the error and the awful thought that another Major was about to get away from him.

Faldo, from the perfect place in the fairway, drilled a four iron to the green and was sitting comfortably 20 feet from the hole. The mechanical man had goaded his rival into error and it looked as though Strange had capitulated when his approach was trapped by the bunker at the green.

It was a deep trap and he stood for a moment looking at the ball as if gathering himself for the most important stroke of his life. Would it be waiting for him this time? Or would his skill desert him when he needed it most? The boisterous fans took time to settle and he was grateful for the respite.

He was not afraid of the shot. Suddenly he was filled with the thought that he had played such bunker shots a thousand times before. It was not difficult. He did not even need a great shot. Just a good one. That realization allowed him the freedom he needed to perform as he knew he could. The ball drifted out through the sand, bobbled, then checked no more than 12 inches from the hole. The crowd erupted with delight.

Now it was Faldo's turn. Strange could only wait and watch as the Englishman's ball was launched towards the hole, looked as though it would stay on line but then strayed towards the right edge and would not come back. They had tied for the championship and would be obliged to return the next day for a play-off over eighteen holes. Strange may have lived to fight another day but he was angry at his errors over the closing stretch.

That night he slept fitfully, unable to banish thoughts of the encounter from his mind. In the match – for that is what it had become between them – the following day, he was slow to settle, missing fairways and leaving himself a succession of middle range putts to save himself. Yet he was still clear of the Englishman after nine holes perhaps because of such infuriating scrambling play. By the thirteenth, Faldo took three putts after being too aggressive with his first attempt as Strange scored a birdie three and went

three strokes clear.

What could possibly go wrong now? Faldo clawed back a stroke on the long fourteenth with a birdie. Now there were only two shots between them. And Strange was bunkered on the next hole while the Englishman reached the edge of the green. If Faldo was going to strike then this was the moment . . . a chip-in perhaps. But instead of the measured swing, the stroke went horribly wrong as it thinned across the green to rough on the other side. It was a staggering mistake from a man who was the epitome of solid consistency. He bogeyed and so did Strange.

Faldo was a beaten man. His approach to the seventeenth was too strong and though Strange was in yet another bunker he came out and saved par to open a three-stroke lead. And just to be absolutely certain he took a two iron from the last tee even though it meant he needed the same club again to reach the green. No matter. The ball arrived on target. Strange was champion at last.

Only then did he think about the old man. And he told the hushed crowds, 'This was for my dad. I've been waiting a long time to do this, to thank the people who gave me the advice I needed, the enthusiasm and the knowledge to continue on. But I just wish my dad could have been here.'

All the people who had helped him along the way knew exactly what he meant. The debt had been repaid. They had all played their part in the making of this champion. They could all share in his glory. Then he was struck by another thought, 'This was my first Major. But we are not going to stop here. We're really not going to stop here.'

Prophetic words from the young man who a year later would successfully defend his US Open and join the legendary Ben Hogan as one of the few golfers ever to achieve it. Not even Jack Nicklaus had managed it. But then Curtis always dreamed that one day he would beat Big Jack. And the old man had got it right . . . there is no ambition that cannot be fulfilled . . .

# CHAPTER EIGHT

# Sandy Lyle and the comeback nobody noticed

It had come down to this. He no longer wanted to play. There was too much humiliation and anguish awaiting him whenever he reached for a club. Yet he knew nothing else. There was no other reason for his life.

From the age of five, Sandy had been given to golf; he had been born to it. He never questioned his destiny nor considered any other vocation. There was a oneness about himself and a golf course which defied analysis; as though he was complete only when he trod the fairways.

If there can be genius in athletic endeavour, then Lyle was close to it. What he did was instinctive – the choice of club, the feel for a shot – and he could never explain the reason afterwards except to say that it was obvious to him.

From childhood he had been earmarked for greatness and it surprised nobody when success came cascading towards him in such volume that at times he could permit himself the most outrageous mistakes on the big occasion and still carry off the title.

That was the measure of his talent; an unquestioned skill that set him far apart from the rest and was so natural that even he could not explain why and how it happened. Nor did there seem any reason to question it.

Not, that is, until the nightmare had begun. The magic had disappeared without warning. There was no reason, no gradual decline. It was as though he woke up one morning and some wicked spell had been cast over him and he could no longer play as he had always done.

The crash had been spectacular, mystifying and well-documented by press and public every miserable inch of the way. Here was a proven champion on the threshold of what promised to be a legendary career. He had captured major titles on both sides of the Atlantic. He was a millionaire. Moreover, he was a sporting hero and a role-model for thousands of youngsters to follow.

Now it was over. And the misery endured.. At first there was sympathy and wise verdicts that, with his natural flair, his game would return as instantly as it had disappeared. Then the brave words grew fainter. He became 'poor old Sandy'. And then nobody bothered

The hardest part of his decline was the memory of how good he had once been and how poor he had now become. Lyle had never questioned his talent but at the 1990 Open at St Andrews, down among the supporting acts, he found the way back. *Phil Sheldon* about him at all. The decline had taken less than a year.

The name and status still meant something of course. Here at St Andrews, he still had a good draw for the Open championship's first two rounds – Tom Kite and Vijay Singh – though neither of them could claim to be a true champion in terms of Sandy's achievements. But it was the best that Lyle could expect.

He suspected he had become an object of curiosity; as though people wanted to see him only to find out if he really was as bad as had been said and perhaps fancifully spot what was wrong with him. In any case he had been deluged with cures and tips from well-meaning fans and admirers but none seemed to work.

He was like a centipede who had suddenly forgotten how to get all his legs moving at once; or rather could not execute the manoeuvre once he thought about it. Worse still, he began to doubt his own individual technique even though it had earned him the British Open and US Masters titles as well as a formidable collection of other trophies around the world.

What bothered him was the frightening speed with which he had lost his touch. It seemed to have happened in the middle of a round on the American tour when he was at the height of his powers, with the best part of $300,000 prize money already in the bank, early in 1989.

True enough the swing had felt a little rusty but, with his kind of style, this feeling was nothing new. And then in Florida, he started well and was toiling efficiently on the second day when a thunderstorm held up play after nine holes. When he resumed, he could no longer play like Sandy Lyle. The nightmare had occurred as simply and as suddenly as that.

Nor would the touch return. The man who had dominated European golf for almost a decade had become a supporting act. His professional pride was so damaged that he began to resent being seen in this state. He even turned down the chance to play in the Ryder Cup against the Americans because he knew he would be picked for what he had been and not what he could contribute to the team in his present state.

And now he was obliged to appear before his 'ain folk' at St Andrews. He had played miserably in the US Masters and the US Open to miss the halfway qualifying score in both events and he knew he would become the target of the press if he were to miss out again on his home territory. Lyle was about to face the most important round of his extraordinary career. And he knew it.

A few days before the event, his caddie, Dave Musgrove, marched round the course, as was his custom, checking the yardages and choosing his own special marks – a bush, a faraway spire, perhaps a water sprinkler – from which to gauge distance or direction to the obscure greens. The process took about four hours and the Midlander liked the solitude it gave him.

The past months had not been easy for him either. He had been a loyal servant of Lyle since 1981 and it was as much a genuine friendship as a boss-employee relationship. They were, in a sense, partners, with the caddie well aware that his role was to be totally supportive and give the golfer the required confidence to play the strokes he needed.

But it occurred to Musgrove as he marched round the Old Course, that perhaps it really was all over and he could no longer inspire Sandy in the way that was necessary. He could neither lift the man's spirits nor restore the essential determination that had left him.

That, in truth, was what had disappeared: Lyle's determination; his willingness to fight for a score even when things went wrong. Sandy was always capable of lurching from the sublime to the ridiculous in a moment, but he always retained the mental fortitude to overcome such lapses and even to laugh at them.

That time at Woburn, for instance, when he hit a seven iron out of bounds on the fourteenth hole. He had just laughed, 'That was a bloody daft shot. We'll just have to make a few more birdies now.' And he did. But not any more. Now the spectacle of a bad lie after an inevitable bad shot brought nothing but gloom and resignation to Lyle.

Worse still, it seemed at times that Sandy simply wanted to get off the course; that his answer to every bad shot was to retreat and hide away on the practice ground as though relentless drilling would iron out such errors when in reality he knew this could never be so.

When Sandy had watched a video of his 1988 victory in the Greater Greensboro Open in North Carolina a week before he won the US Masters he had scoffed, 'God, look at that swing. How awful.'

Musgrove had countered, 'Aye, but who did they give the cheque to? Who won?' It saddened him that Lyle had been transformed from that free, uninhibited athlete into a timorous, yet fussy, performer for whom every joint in his body had to be in textbook position before he was satisfied the stroke could be correct.

As they stood on the practice ground for yet another protracted session, Musgrove pointed to the Old Course and said, 'That's where the championship is going to be played. Not here. Let's play a few more holes.' And he was relieved when Lyle agreed although he had more or less come to the conclusion that, if this week ended in yet another failure, he would tell his boss it was time to get a new caddie – for his own good.

Lyle himself had already come to the conclusion that whatever the original reason for his decline, his confidence was now in pieces. He expected the worst and was rarely disappointed. And yet the most infuriating aspect of his present state was that it revealed the narrowness of the margin that exists between good and bad golf.

For most of his life, it had all seemed so straightforward, perhaps even easy. In the manner of child prodigy, he had been protected from the outside world and more specifically from anything which might interfere with his art. Others took the decisions away from the fairways and Sandy was happy to comply.

It had endured into manhood with his father, Alex, the club professional

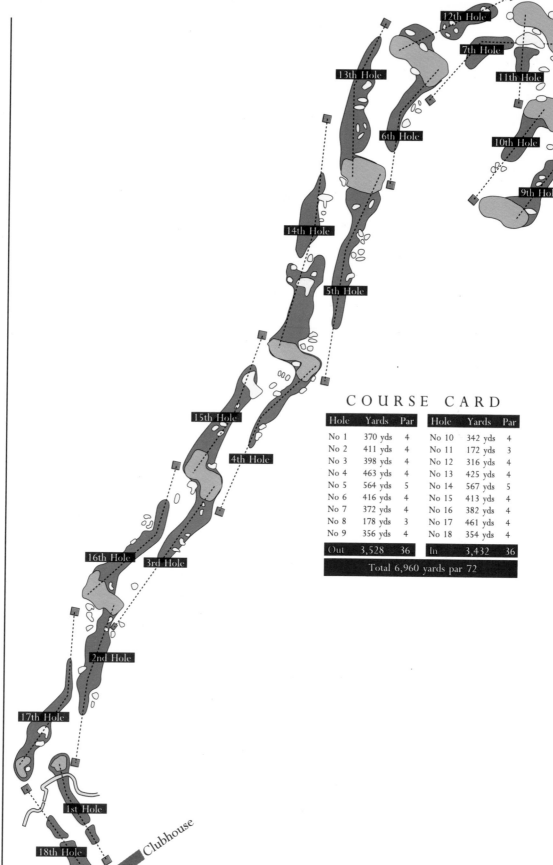

# St Andrews

12th Hole

7th Hole

13th Hole

11th Hole

8th H

6th Hole

10th Hole

9th Hole

14th Hole

5th Hole

## COURSE CARD

| Hole | Yards | Par | | Hole | Yards | Par |
|------|-------|-----|---|------|-------|-----|
| No 1 | 370 yds | 4 | | No 10 | 342 yds | 4 |
| No 2 | 411 yds | 4 | | No 11 | 172 yds | 3 |
| No 3 | 398 yds | 4 | | No 12 | 316 yds | 4 |
| No 4 | 463 yds | 4 | | No 13 | 425 yds | 4 |
| No 5 | 564 yds | 5 | | No 14 | 567 yds | 5 |
| No 6 | 416 yds | 4 | | No 15 | 413 yds | 4 |
| No 7 | 372 yds | 4 | | No 16 | 382 yds | 4 |
| No 8 | 178 yds | 3 | | No 17 | 461 yds | 4 |
| No 9 | 356 yds | 4 | | No 18 | 354 yds | 4 |
| Out | 3,528 | 36 | | In | 3,432 | 36 |
| Total 6,960 yards par 72 | | | | | | |

15th Hole

4th Hole

16th Hole

3rd Hole

2nd Hole

17th Hole

1st Hole

Clubhouse

18th Hole

At his peak, it had all seemed so easy for Lyle who had learned to play as a toddler. In 1988 when he won the US Masters title, he was acknowledged to be one of the most exciting players in the world. *Karina Hoskyns/Phil Sheldon*

from Shropshire where Sandy grew up, in complete control. There was that time at the US Masters when Alex told him to get his hair cut and then sent him back again because it wasn't short enough.

There had been, too, that enduring rivalry with Nick Faldo as they chased and swapped titles through boyhood and into manhood, although both of them knew in those early days that Faldo judged himself against Sandy and saw him as the target.

They were, of course, diverse characters from differing backgrounds. Sandy had been born to golf and knew nothing else. Faldo had come to it in his teens and, while Sandy had been graced with a casual talent, Faldo had toiled relentlessly to acquire his technique and then later in life was to scrap it all and start again.

If what existed between them was a race to become the dominant figure in the British game, then Sandy seemed to have won it convincingly, first by capturing the British Open, the first home player since Tony Jacklin in 1969 to do so, when he even indulged in a fluffed chip shot to the last green at Royal St George's as he won in 1985.

And then, while Faldo was engaged in the anonymous tribulations of reassembling his golf swing under the vigilant eye of tutor David Leadbetter, Sandy captured the Tournament Players championship in Florida and later took the US Masters at Augusta in the most gloriously casual style.

That had been vintage Lyle stuff as he toyed with the prospect of failure even until the last moment as his tee shot finished in a bunker to the left of the steep uphill last fairway from where he crushed a seven iron approach to the green, then holed the putt for a winning birdie.

In that moment, what was it? Skill? Most certainly. Confidence? Most definitely. Determination? Most assuredly. And where had it gone? And why?

Lyle had read all the gratuitous analysis of his decline: the first marriage that had failed and with it the loss in real terms – despite visiting rights – of his two sons. They would, after all, not grow up in his household. His vagabond lifestyle, despite its millionaire trimmings around the world, was too much of a price to pay. Yet for him, it was the only life he knew.

And so the theory grew that perhaps it was this first devastating brush with the harsh facts of life that had dealt Sandy's confidence the savage blow that was to remove all purpose from him on the golf course – his place of work and by definition the supposed cause of the family break-up. It was a neat theory. But it was false.

Most of his great success had come when he knew his marriage was over. True, he had already won the British Open and was at the 1986 US Masters when his first wife, Christine, told him it was over between them. Yet in the next two years he won the American Players championship as well as the US Masters and the World Matchplay titles among a total of six prestigious events.

No, as sad as that break-up had been

in his life, it was not the reason for the decline and certainly not when Jolande, a Dutch physiotherapist whom he had met on tour during this low period, was there to support him and eventually became his wife.

There had to be some other reason because this was more than just the ebb and flow of form that every player experiences; more, too, than even protracted rustiness which has assailed all the great players – from Henry Cotton to Jack Nicklaus – but from which they all emerged to triumph again.

It was on the practice ground at St Andrews before the first round that Lyle was to meet a man who would bring about the first real signs of change; the faint glimmer of hope that he really could find a way back to his past brilliance no matter how long it took.

Noel Blundell, a sports psychologist, accepts that among people of equal technical ability at the very top of a sport, the only difference between winners and losers is their mental attitude; the confidence to achieve what their technique most certainly will allow if only their minds will permit.

Perhaps the limiting factor is simply the fear of failure; the awareness of what can go wrong because it has happened so often in the past. In Lyle's case he had taken the process a stage farther. He had begun to doubt the technique; begun to blame it for his ills when it had worked well enough to take him to a position of pre-eminence in the world of golf.

Clearly Lyle needed to be distracted from the preoccupation with his technique so that he could concentrate instead on the job in hand of putting together a good score which, after all, is the primary purpose of all the practice and swing disciplines. Somehow Lyle had mislaid that priority.

'When you aim at the green, concentrate on the flag and not just any part of it. Make sure you focus at the lower bit by the hole. That is after all where the ball must go in the end.' There were other mental exercises, too, which the psychologist passed on to Lyle during the mornings that they met on the practice ground and which had the effect of distracting him from what he perceived to be his own inadequacies.

Moreover, it seemed to be working. Not spectacularly enough for anybody to sit up and take notice, of course. The cruel irony was that Faldo, who had lived in his shadow and whom he had beaten to most of the glittering prizes, was now the main attraction, hailed as the man most likely to succeed and the focus of media and public attention. He was already twice US Masters champion, a runner-up in the US Open as well as being a former British Open champion. He had arrived in St Andrews as clear favourite for the title.

From the first hole however, Sandy knew this was not going to be a free-flowing, effortless performance but would instead require all the grit and determination that had once been the hallmark of his play; qualities, in fact, whose absence perhaps were the causes of his decline not the effect of it.

He drilled a one iron from the first

# A ROUND TO REMEMBER

When he sank the putt to become US Masters champion, there was no suspicion that this brilliant form would vanish so quickly and mysteriously. For a while at least, Sandy could be the happiest golfer in the world.
*Karina Hoskyns/Phil Sheldon*

Two years later, the crowds still applaud as he walks off the green in the 1990 Open at St Andrews. But this time, he is no longer a winner but a confused man determined to find his way back. *Karina Hoskyns/Phil Sheldon*

tee just short of the burn then wedged a reasonable distance from the flag for what seemed a gentle but confident introduction. But then unaccountably he three-putted to revive fears of the old nightmare. And yet this time he held himself together and toiled relentlessly to sign his name to a level par 72.

Yet he knew this meant he could not afford any errors on the second day because the experts had predicted the halfway qualifying score would be around level par – in fact it turned out to be one under par – which meant Lyle had to produce another score no worse than his first display.

All those electrifying Lyle scores, when it had all seemed so easy, mattered not one jot now. The man who could shoot 63 in a storm-lashed French Open now faced what had become for him the monumental task of scoring 71 at worst to make sure of his place in the final two rounds. There had never been a more important round in the career of Sandy Lyle.

And it began in crisis. He reached for the one iron to start his second round, just as he had done on the previous day, but he had failed to notice the strength of the wind had changed so that it now gusted from behind him. Unerringly, the ball disappeared into the burn 290 yards away from the tee.

This was the disaster he had feared. He dropped out under penalty then wedged rather disconsolately 30 feet from the flagstick for what seemed a damaging opening bogey. Then, quite outrageously, he drilled the ball into the hole for an impudent par four that was to lift his spirits higher than any birdie could have done.

On the second hole, he knew the ideal ploy was to land the approach shot a few yards short of the green and let the ball run up and on to the putting surface towards the flag. He hit what he thought was a perfect shot and, as they clambered over the humps and hollows, was dismayed when he heard Musgrove growl, 'The bastard's short.'

True enough, the ball had failed to carry to the green. Even so, Sandy seemed unruffled. He simply chipped and putted to save his par. And suddenly his caddie realized the old Lyle was back. The chin jutted out in determined fashion. There was that critical glint in his eye as he watched the ball fly through the air and come to earth. He had fought and earned his pars on the first two holes and that seemed to make him more determined. He had found his sense of purpose again.

With a following wind, the wise and customary strategy is to attempt to make a good score on the outward holes if for no other reason than insurance against the homeward struggle into the wind over more difficult terrain. Sandy went his own way, typically snatching birdies on two of the most difficult holes on the course – the thirteenth and the fifteenth – then steered a diligent route through the treacherous seventeenth Road Hole.

Now he faced the final drive. Not a winner, of course. But that did not matter to the thousands of jubilant fans who thronged the last green, and waved from the windows of every building flanking the final fairway. The cheers were for glories past, of course. But it seemed too that they sensed the intensity of the personal struggle Sandy was about to win; the personal battle for survival – not just in this important contest – that had been put before him.

So they roared as he walked on to the green and holed out for a 70 and a place in the final two rounds among the supporting cast. Time was when he would have topped the leaderboard but, for now, this would do. If nothing else, it was a sign that there really was a road back to glory for Lyle. He knew for certain now that the old determination and fire still simmered within him.

It mattered not that Faldo became champion again. All power and credit to him. At least Sandy was to make the front line of the chorus to finish in sixteenth place. It had been a personal victory he thought he would never win. Perhaps the most important of his life. It had gone unnoticed by all except those who were close to him and knew the turmoil he had endured. It was the day he learned he had not lost the gift of golf for ever; and that he could once again stand on the first tee in hope rather than fear. All in all, a famous victory. And one of the most secret too.

# CHAPTER NINE

# Bernhard Langer and the power of prayer

When he arrived at the church, the door was locked. Odd really, for a Sunday morning. Langer felt he needed to pray because of what lay ahead of him that day. And now his good intention had been foiled.

In a sense, his life had been a preparation for this moment. All the toil and hardship, the dreams and ambitions had been focused on what was about to occur. He had not known where or when it would happen; only that some day the chance to step from the crowd and become a champion would present itself.

And now it was here. It was a frightening prospect; not just the process of trying to win the US Masters with all the tension and dramas, crises and errors that entailed but rather the irrevocable transformation that would take place in his life as a result. Nothing would ever be the same again.

Could he do it? Or had he just been deluding himself with day-dreams that had no basis for substance? Yet, surely each great champion had been obliged at some point to take this awesome step out of the cosiness of the ordinary and undemanding existence in the supporting ranks.

Maybe such a step stood in the lives of many people of obvious gifts and abilities who were to find sadly they could not accomplish it. Nobody could ever really be sure how a champion is made and more importantly whether the essential qualities lay dormant within him.

It was all very confusing, which is why Langer felt the need for a spiritual moment in the sanctuary of a church. But here on Washington Road, only a few yards from the Augusta National course where his future was about to be decided, the door was bolted.

He turned to his American wife, Vikki, and suggested they went back to the house they had rented for the week. They would simply pray together there until it was time to go to the course.

He had never been coy about the importance of prayer. While others, particularly Gary Player, had always insisted they prayed only to do their best – not simply to win – Bernhard made no secret of the fact that he asked the Almighty to give him success on the fairways. Life

Langer admitted that at times he felt intimidated by Ballesteros yet regarded him as the man to beat. It was the sweetest moment of his life when the Spaniard acknowledged defeat in the 1985 US Masters as Bernhard outplayed him to become champion. *Phil Sheldon* itself was a challenge in which every achievement was a victory of sorts.

What, then, was wrong with praying for sporting success? And yet that Sunday morning, he had a more specific request in mind. He was thankful to be among the leaders with a chance of victory but, above all else, he wanted two things on this most important day of his life. He wanted to remain calm. And he wanted to be in control of himself. For this, Langer prayed.

Two days earlier he had been chatting in the rented house with his golf coach, Willi Hoffman, and a German television producer who asked him what were his ambitions and goals for the week. A reasonable question really, considering Langer was two over par and six strokes behind the halfway leader and destined, it seemed, merely to be playing for place money and no greater prize.

'I think I can win it', Langer declared. The producer was too polite to laugh and too loyal to argue. But he remained unconvinced. What he had failed to realize was that Langer had considered all the angles, possibilities as well as the calibre and form of those ahead of him, and had come to the conclusion that it really was possible for him to win. Moreover he never made a statement unless he meant it.

It is the private, almost spiritual, nature of golf that at times a player senses he is playing well even before his scores reflect it. To the outsider, Langer was not at his best. Two weeks earlier in the Tournament Players Championship in Florida, his swing had suddenly lost its rhythmic efficiency and he was struggling to regain it.

His scores after the first two rounds at Augusta suggested he was still toiling to find the touch. And yet Langer was invariably at his best when things against him were at their worst. He had more than a nodding acquaintance with hardship and adversity. They did not frighten him.

Even at that moment, he could reflect on a life that had always required painstaking effort and plenty of it. In childhood, he was not gifted nor did he come from an affluent background. His mother, Wally, worked in a local cafe. His father, Erwin, was a bricklayer. Langer himself had started work at the local golf club as a boy caddie to make extra money for the family.

He was by nature a solitary character and one who seemed to prefer his own company or rather did not feel compelled constantly to seek out others. It was a resolute disposition inherited from his father Erwin who towards the end of the Second World War jumped from a train that was taking military prisoners to the USSR and an uncertain fate.

After working for months on remote farms and living in barns to escape being recaptured he arrived quietly in the town of Anhausen. He found a job then met and married a local waitress. They had three children Erwin, Maria and the youngest, Bernhard, all of whom worked at the local Augsburg Golf Club on a part-time basis to make money. It was a lifestyle that held little prospect beyond their own modest town nor did they seek more.

It was young Bernhard's quickening talent for golf that led to an awareness of the outside world. By the time he was fifteen, he had become good enough to be offered a job as an assistant professional at the Munich Golf Club, almost a two-hour journey from his home. There were, however, strict conditions. He had to reside near the club and would be allowed home only once every six weeks. He would be obliged to learn English and to attend a business studies school as well as working at the club.

Thus did the lonely pilgrimage of Bernhard Langer begin. It was to be a slow journey in which progress and success were hard-earned yet in consequence solidly based. By the time he was nineteen he had decided he wanted to be a tournament player and the great adventure began in an old Ford Escort which he drove 1,600 miles on a round trip from Germany to southern Spain and Portugal.

These were the days of life on the breadline; of sleeping in cheap and tawdry lodgings; of lying awake with the bedroom lights left on to enable him to see the insects and bugs. It was not the life of glamour he had in mind. Moreover he was beset suddenly by another problem which should have halted his career even before it started.

He was assailed by a putting twitch, an affliction traditionally thought to be brought on by pressure and strain over a long period and therefore generally to be found only in competitors who have played for many years and whose nerve has simply been frayed by time itself.

Never had it been found in a young man. Not until Langer came along.

It manifests itself in a sudden spasm of the hands before the putt is made. In that moment of tranquillity before the stroke, suddenly the hands jerk into unwanted action and the ball is struck erratically. It is a condition which has afflicted even the great golfers down the years. The legendary Harry Vardon became a sufferer in his declining years. So, too, did Ben Hogan. The distinguished golf essayist, Henry Longhurst, himself a sufferer, concluded, 'Once you've had 'em, you've got 'em!' To him, there was no respite except to give up the game completely.

The problem for Langer probably began on the lush, slow greens of Augsburg where he learned to play and upon which the ball had to be struck firmly towards the hole to overcome the strongly resistant grass. However once Bernard was introduced to the specially prepared fast greens of the professional circuit, he discovered his stroke was too forceful and, lacking the essential finesse, he was beset by a constant fear every time he stepped to a putt. The inevitable result of this struggle for control of his nerve was that his hands would shudder in spasm – especially on the short putts.

And yet, he was determined to overcome the problem and devised a series of first-aid remedies – from alternative putters to various putting grips including the cack-handed left-hand-below-right method to keep his problem in control. In this respect, the ultimate achievement of his career would be to become merely an

# A ROUND TO REMEMBER

He had endured a lifetime struggle with his putting yet it was the high quality of his golf and the constant help of his personal coach, Willi Hoffman, as they prepared for the 1985 US Masters title attempt that saw him through.
*Phil Sheldon*

average putter and when this happened, by grinding hard work, it supported his superlative golf swing well enough to make him a tournament winner.

Inevitably he became regarded as one of the bright stars of European golf as it moved to the centre of the world stage. Alternatively he was viewed as either the arch-rival to Seve Ballesteros or as a member of the invading force which threatened the rising British stars, Nick Faldo, Sandy Lyle and Ian Woosnam. It was all good show-business and gave the sport itself more box-office appeal.

And yet for Bernhard, Seve had always been the target. They were of similar age but when Bernhard struggled to finish in ninetieth place in the European money list of 1976, Seve was already a star and leading money winner, a position he was to hold for the next three years during which he won eleven tournaments including the 1979 Open championship at Royal Lytham and St Annes.

By that time, Bernard had inched up towards forty-fifth in the money list with only an Under-25 title to his credit. Ballesteros hardly noticed he was there yet the gap was closing between them so that by 1981 Langer himself had taken over as top money winner and in so doing earned himself a job that was to sour his relationship with Ballesteros for several years.

As top money winner, Bernhard was involved in picking the Ryder Cup team to play the Americans, along with the then Chairman of the European Tour, Neil Coles, and the Ryder Cup captain, John Jacobs. Between them they drop-ped Seve from the side. The conclusion drawn – though never proved – was that Bernhard must have had the casting vote because skipper Jacobs must have wanted Ballesteros, then the world's best golfer, in his team, but Chairman Coles would have demurred if only because the Spaniard had been arguing about appearance money demands from sponsors to the disquiet of other professionals.

It had been an unwise selection set-up to have one player obliged to sit in judgement of another and in a year when Ballesteros finished seventh in the money list, winning two tournaments, he could rightfully be regarded amongst the top twelve players needed to play for Europe against the Americans.

The decision smacked of censure; of lessons being taught and of having little to do with the best interests of the team; although some Ryder Cup candidates were fiercely opposed to Seve being selected. Only a subsequent change of selection rules and the persuasive powers of a new skipper, Tony Jacklin, managed to entice Seve back into the side to launch what was to be an era of historic success.

But, at the time, the collective decision to leave Seve out of the 1981 Cup squad was to give a sharp edge to their relationship and a deeper significance whenever they clashed on a golf course. On the eve of their encounter in the 1984 World Matchplay Championship at Wentworth, Bernhard had told an astounded press corps that he did not like playing with Seve because he found him to be 'intimidating'.

It had been the wrong choice of word

because it implied that the Spaniard was guilty of antics that came close to gamesmanship. What he had meant to say was that Seve existed in a world of his own when he was on the golf course. Nobody else mattered. Not even his opponent. He talked very little, rarely praised a good shot and had an irritating habit of practising his putting just within view of an opponent who was about to putt.

When Seve was told what Langer had said that day, he was astounded and angered. The remarks led to a renewal of the coolness that existed between them and also resulted in an embarrassing and public confrontation in the press room after the Spaniard had triumphed by 2 and 1 at Wentworth.

In front of pressmen Seve demanded to know what his rival had meant by his remarks but Langer insisted he had not meant to be critical but that his words if anything were intended to be complimentary to the Spaniard's powers of concentration. Later both men would talk more deeply and in private about the nature of their rivalry and how personal it had become.

But now, as Langer made his way to Augusta for the final round of the 1985 US Masters, six months after that confrontation with Seve at Wentworth, he reflected on the vagaries of the drawsheet that had paired them together for this final day. Both had a chance of victory although Augusta was already being regarded as the Spaniard's personal domain in the way it had belonged to Jack Nicklaus in his prime. Seve was clearly the man to beat.

Langer found himself two strokes behind the tournament leader, Ray Floyd, and one stroke behind Curtis Strange as they prepared for the final round. He had promised himself he would not look at the scoreboard during that day because he wanted no distractions and anyway he had no control over what anybody else was doing.

He had already felt justified with his decision to change his complete set of irons after the first two rounds, even though some thought he was running a serious risk of losing his touch in the middle of this contest. In fact the effect had been to transform his play.

Of course there had been some good fortune too. Nothing is ever achieved without it. A day earlier, he knew he had to force the pace and take chances if he was to get closer to the lead. Such thinking prompted him to take a chance on the formidable thirteenth hole when common sense told him he should play short of the creek that runs across the fairway in front of the green.

Instead, he had decided to go for it with a four wood even though his ball lay in semi-rough. He struck it perfectly then watched anxiously as it soared then dropped sickeningly short of the creek but miraculously bounced over and skidded to a halt 20 feet from the flagstick. He holed the putt for an eagle three and had established himself among the contenders.

As he walked to the first tee, Langer kept telling himself not to watch Seve as they played. He must think only of his own game. One shot at a time. No thinking ahead; no fanciful thoughts about what one crucial putt could do to his scorecard. But, above all, don't look at the leaderboards.

By the ninth hole he gave in to the temptation and immediately wished he had not done so. He could not believe how well Curtis Strange was doing. The American had opened a four-stroke lead with only nine holes to play. It was then that Langer resolved simply to try the best he could and if that meant finishing in twentieth place then so be it.

Quite suddenly, he felt an extraordinary calm come over him. For some unaccountable reason he found himself in complete control and the thought surprised him. It was as though he had just stumbled upon this priceless gift and there was no explanation. More to the point, he was struck by what seemed an outrageous thought. If he could play the homeward nine – arguably the most treacherous stretch in all of golf – in four under par, he could still win. There were hard holes still to be played and for Strange it would not be easy trying to hold on over that territory.

He knew the exact moment when Seve ceased to be a threat – perhaps even before the Spaniard himself realized it. He began to moan and groan at his caddie in the most colourful terms when strokes and putts missed their intended target. It was a sure sign that all was not well for Ballesteros.

Then Langer sensed another significant change. He birdied the notorious short twelfth hole across Rae's Creek and somehow detected a buzz of anticipation from the crowd. Their mood told him he was getting closer. But how close? Should he look at the leaderboard? Maybe he was already in the lead. What then? Play safe? No. Better not to know. He had come this far in ignorance. Why change?

His refusal to seek such intelligence meant he did not know that Strange had suffered disasters and played the long thirteenth and fifteenth holes in ruinous fashion to drop strokes when he should have been gaining them. Meanwhile Langer, the man who had been dismissed so early in his career as an incurable yipper of putts, was in superlative form on greens that by common consent were regarded as the most difficult and frightening to play because of their pace and contours.

By the time he had snapped up birdie putts on the thirteenth and the fifteenth holes, Langer knew instinctively the balance of the game was changing. There had been no roars from other parts of the course to signal that the crowds had seen other birdie putts being holed. He must be clear of them all by now.

From the middle of the seventeenth fairway he despatched the ball with an eight iron some 14 feet from the flagstick and then holed the putt for yet another birdie. He had reached the predicted four under par on the back nine that he thought he would need to win. Now was the time to see if it was good enough. He looked at the leaderboard. He was two strokes clear of the entire field.

Seve, no longer the rival though he had stayed within menacing reach until

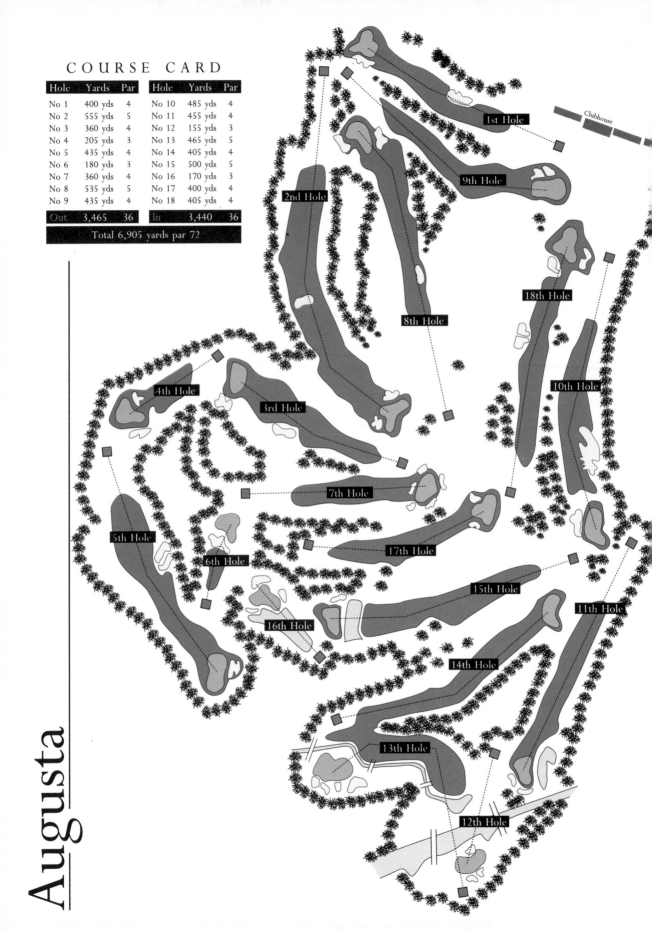

COURSE CARD

| Hole | Yards | Par | Hole | Yards | Par |
|------|-------|-----|------|-------|-----|
| No 1 | 400 yds | 4 | No 10 | 485 yds | 4 |
| No 2 | 555 yds | 5 | No 11 | 455 yds | 4 |
| No 3 | 360 yds | 4 | No 12 | 155 yds | 3 |
| No 4 | 205 yds | 3 | No 13 | 465 yds | 5 |
| No 5 | 435 yds | 4 | No 14 | 405 yds | 4 |
| No 6 | 180 yds | 3 | No 15 | 500 yds | 5 |
| No 7 | 360 yds | 4 | No 16 | 170 yds | 3 |
| No 8 | 535 yds | 5 | No 17 | 400 yds | 4 |
| No 9 | 435 yds | 4 | No 18 | 405 yds | 4 |
| Out | 3,465 | 36 | In | 3,440 | 36 |
| | | Total 6,905 yards par 72 | | | |

Clubhouse

1st Hole
9th Hole
2nd Hole
8th Hole
18th Hole
10th Hole
4th Hole
3rd Hole
5th Hole
7th Hole
6th Hole
17th Hole
15th Hole
11th Hole
16th Hole
14th Hole
13th Hole
12th Hole

Augusta

He had forced himself not to look at the leaderboards as he started the final day in case he was distracted or intimidated. But when he knew he was clear not even a bunker on the last hole could shake his confidence. *Phil Sheldon*

the sixteenth green, came over and patted him on the shoulder as they stood on the eighteenth tee. He said simply, 'Well played. You've got it.'

Langer was not so sure. It was not yet over. One hole of Augusta, especially the last, was all it required to turn certain victory into the worst possible kind of defeat. In 1961 Arnold Palmer came up the last hole acknowledging the cheers of the crowd as the obvious new champion and then, from the middle of the fairway, took a nightmarish six to lose the title to Gary Player who was already in the clubhouse watching the astonishing drama on television.

Langer's caution was well placed. He dropped a stroke on the final green which gave faint but fading hope to the unfortunate Strange who failed to force a play-off. When it was over and Langer knew he was champion, the words of Ballesteros, his old rival, remained with him.

'Well done. You played very well. You deserved to win,' said Seve. 'I am happy that it was one of us Europeans that won – and not one of them.' A pointed reference to the American professionals who did not figure highly on Seve's list of people he admired.

Thus, the transformation was complete. Langer had joined that élite band of champions. The trappings of success were apparent. The green jacket, symbol of club membership and so much more. Even his own locker in a special room of the clubhouse where no one else except the champions could enter.

All the old demons had been laid to rest. Any doubts about his own worth, identity and ability with a putter had vanished. For his wife, Vikki, it was a pivotal moment too. She was in tears and when Langer asked her afterwards why she was crying, she said that his triumph meant they could now start the family they had always wanted. At last, they were financially secure!

For Bernhard, there was no time to think. There were interviews to be done for the press and television. There was a special dinner with a club official to attend. Then on to a party with some Australian friends who had won a lot of money as a result of his win. When he got back to his room he could not sleep. The events of the day were recalled and savoured. Even his past life rushed before him – the childhood days at Augsburg; the clattering round Europe in his cheap car via cheap hotels; the struggles against his putting; the traumas and triumphs with Seve. They had all led to this moment. They had to be recalled and remembered in private. They belonged to a past life. This was a new beginning.

# CHAPTER TEN

# Rodger Davis and the milkman's best round

As soon as he hit the ball, he wanted to break into a run to see how close it had finished to the flagstick. But Davis fought the urge and instead inhaled deeply a couple of times and marched onwards at a measured pace.

This was no time to reveal the turmoil within himself; the frightening realization that he was as close as he had ever been to stepping out of the ranks to become a champion.

One thing was certain. It would be over in the next few minutes and either Des Smyth or himself would earn the title of PGA champion and take a rightful place in the record books. It would soon be part of the history of the game for ever; a fixture for all time.

He was not normally given to such profound insights or to dwelling on the broader view of life. Since those early times when he delivered milk bottles by night in a Sydney suburb and worked in a pro shop by day, there was always some pressing job to hand; always something to be done next and never time to look up and see where it was taking him.

But Rodger also knew there had always

been a question-mark over him; or rather, perhaps more than most, he felt an obligation to prove his worth as a professional golfer that went beyond simply gaining recognition in an already overcrowded world of Australian stars that included Greg Norman, David Graham and Graham Marsh.

A psychologist might have traced this crusade back to his amateur days in New South Wales and the bitter disappointment he felt when he was rejected for the Australian team for the Eisenhower Trophy, even though he was then one of the best amateur golfers in his country.

The ways and means of selectors are always mysterious, often hurtful, but for Davis, who had been an outstanding candidate, they defied explanation and hurt him so deeply that he turned professional immediately.

At twenty-three, it was a risk. He was an extremely late starter in one of the toughest careers in professional sport. He was married, with one child and another on the way and he was about to throw up a well-paid job with prospects in an oil company. But then Davis was never

It was the moment Davis knew all the hard work and determination had been justified. He had overcome all the odds and earned the accolade of PGA champion at Wentworth in 1986. *Phil Sheldon* daunted by the size of the task but was rather more concerned with how long it would take to complete.

Moreover, it would be done his way. When he told friends at Pemble Golf Club that he was going to give up his career as an analyst and turn professional, they had offered to sponsor him, but he refused. He was taking the risk and he wanted all the rewards. He wanted no help from anybody.

For a punishing year, that decision had meant a relentless treadmill of starting work at midnight, delivering 280 gallons in milk bottles to homes plus another 230 gallons to shops and restaurants before finishing at 7 a.m., then driving the milk van to the golf club to open the shop at 7.30 and working through until 6 p.m.

By 6.15 p.m. he was home and his wife, Pam, had his meal on the table. By 6.45 p.m. he was in bed and asleep and less than five hours later he was awake, dressed and driving the van back to the dairy to load up and start his milk round again. Nobody had to tell Davis what it meant to suffer for one's art. He was paying the price.

Even so, there was a sureness about his attitude which convinced him that life – particularly in golf – was merely an equation in which success was the inevitable consequence of the amount of work done. His first step therefore, had been to earn the cash to support a family so he could then devote himself full-time to professional golf. The rest would follow.

And it had worked. As soon as he joined the Australian circuit after

He had come too far to let it all slip away from him as he faced Irishman Des Smyth in the play-off. But their encounter almost drifted into farce before Davis could lay hands on the title. *Phil Sheldon*

The tally of strokes on that seventeenth hole began to look embarrassing as Davis hacked out of the trees and was still off the green with his fourth stroke. But he chipped and putted for a bogey six to become champion. *Phil Sheldon*

serving his apprenticeship, he began to win money. Within three years he had won three titles and was an established performer. And if the beginnings on the European circuit were rather slow and lacked spectacular impact then at least he paid his expenses and gained experience with every season that passed.

And yet somehow it had all seemed too easy. No, that wasn't quite the word. It was as though he felt no different in approach and attitude to his first-or-nowhere days of carefree amateur golf. There ought to be more to being a professional than simply the titles. But Rodger could not detect that difference in himself.

Not that it seemed to matter as the money and success rolled in with sufficient volume to allow him to invest in land and properties back in Australia. He could also win tournaments in decent company and in 1981 had experienced the first taste of what it was like to prevail over the calibre of star in whose league he secretly suspected he was not.

There had been more to it than just the satisfaction and adulation that came with such triumph. Rather, it was the actual process of winning – the memory afterwards of the strokes played that would never be forgotten. Even now, he could still recall the surprise he felt when he struck his three wood to the last green of that State Express tournament at The Belfry in 1981.

That time, they were all present – Seve Ballesteros and Greg Norman – but there he was with the chance of victory if only he could deliver the ball 230 yards across the lake to the green. It was no time for caution and yet what astonished him as he swung at the ball was that he never felt the impact – never felt it leaving the clubface and even wondered if he had missed it altogether.

Not so. The ball soared to the back of the green and Davis tidied up the formalities with his putter to take first prize. If the secret of successful golf lies in self-knowledge of both weaknesses and strengths, then Davis learned that day that he could deliver the perfect stroke when nothing less would do. It was a thought that was to see him through the troubled and disastrous times ahead when his life, fortune and career seemed to be shattered.

It all went wrong with a good idea. He was tired of being separated from his family in Australia while he pursued success on the European circuit. It was time to go home, watch the children grow up and play his golf on his own national professional circuit.

Better still, he would invest in business to provide a steady source of income. In 1982, he agreed to buy a motel in Budreim, on the magnificent Sunshine Coast some 120 kilometres north of Brisbane. He should have checked the deal more thoroughly because it was not quite what it seemed and the decision to buy was to cost him virtually all that he possessed.

The realities of the balance sheet worked so savagely against him that there was no way to survive financially – no light at the end of the tunnel – unless he went into receivership. Rodger Davis was broke. The man who had found life and golf so well-ordered and predictable had got it wrong and he was obliged to sell off all his investments – even his original home – to pay off the debts.

It was time to start all over again with nothing. And once the initial shock, hurt and anguish had subsided, suddenly the old fire and determination returned. He knew what would be involved in a new beginning and all the sacrifice and effort he would need to build a new life. The feeling was not new. It had been like that when he left the oil company to be a milkman and a golfer. In any case, the other choice was to surrender and wonder for the rest of his life about what-might-have-been.

Thus did Rodger Davis's second and real career in professional golf begin. What had gone before was a casual demonstration of athletic skill. What ensued was a means of survival; the only way he knew to get through his life. And it showed.

He was a hungry golfer in every sense of the word. He needed the cash but equally urgently he needed the success to prove to himself that he was not a failure. A totally new philosophy began to develop in which golf was no longer a sport simply to be enjoyed but rather a business that required all the dedication and expertise to be worked properly.

He coolly assessed his personal balance sheet. He recognized the strengths of his game and knew he had to practise harder on them because they were the features on which any success had to be built. The weaknesses could not be ignored. Work

*Even before he assembled with Des Smyth for the play-off, Davis sensed he had the makings of a champion when he holed from 30 feet on the last green to tie the Irishman and face him over extra holes for the title.* Phil Sheldon

# Wentworth

10th Hole

9th Hole

12th Hole

13th Hole

8th Hole

11th Hole

7th Hole

14th Hole

6th Hole

5th Hole

15th Hole

4th Hole

16th Hole

3rd Hole

17th Hole

2nd Hole

1st Hole

18th Hole

## COURSE CARD

| Hole | Yards | Par | Hole | Yards | Par |
|------|-------|-----|------|-------|-----|
| No 1 | 471 yds | 4 | No 10 | 186 yds | 3 |
| No 2 | 155 yds | 3 | No 11 | 376 yds | 4 |
| No 3 | 452 yds | 4 | No 12 | 483 yds | 5 |
| No 4 | 501 yds | 5 | No 13 | 441 yds | 4 |
| No 5 | 191 yds | 3 | No 14 | 179 yds | 3 |
| No 6 | 344 yds | 4 | No 15 | 466 yds | 4 |
| No 7 | 399 yds | 4 | No 16 | 380 yds | 4 |
| No 8 | 398 yds | 4 | No 17 | 571 yds | 5 |
| No 9 | 450 yds | 4 | No 18 | 502 yds | 5 |
| Out | 3,361 | 35 | In | 3,584 | 37 |
| Total 6,945 yards par 72 | | | | | |

Clubhouse

had to be done on them but his strategy would always be to play to his strength.

He began to concentrate on his short game. Not a day would pass in his life thereafter when he did not hit at least 100 putts in practice and a similar number of chip shots – no matter how late in the day or how tired he felt.

And there was more to be done. When the financial crash came, he had been devastated and might well have toppled into an abyss of self-pity had not two close friends, Don Parrish and Peter Oakley, both Australian rugby league stars, taken control. They decided it was time for Rodger to get fit. For seven weeks, they trained him hard every day, running up and down sandhills on the beach until the podgy Davis had lost 28 lbs and felt strong enough to cope with all the practice he needed to get himself ready for a return to tournament golf.

There was to be greater purpose to his play; a much fiercer attitude to the business of earning money from golf in that a stroke saved meant more money at the end of the week, which in turn meant there was never any excuse to give up trying because even fiftieth place had to be better and pay more than fifty-first. That, too, bred a degree of professionalism that Davis realized had been missing from those early years even when he was winning.

After a hesitant return in 1985, he had found his formidable stride a year later. His form was relentless, rarely out of the top five in Australia and winning the Victoria Open. It was as though he was desperately anxious to make up for lost

time while simultaneously restoring his fortune and pride.

And yet if he was honest with himself, he knew he needed a victory in a prestigious international tournament against the obligatory assembly of superstars to underline not only his comeback but also to measure his own worth in the world of golf.

And now it was here as he walked the last fairway of the West Course at Wentworth. It had been a frenzied day in which he had seen his lead of two strokes disappear so that now he trailed by a stroke to the genial Irishman, Des Smyth, as they marched side by side towards the climax of a championship that had been previously won by Arnold Palmer, Tony Jacklin, Seve Ballesteros and Nick Faldo.

This could now be the biggest blow of all; to let this title slip away when it had been within his grasp. He had steadfastly held on to all the mental and physical tricks he had been advised would help him cope with the pressures and maintain his concentration – the manner of focusing precisely on an object at which to aim to the exclusion of all else; the obligation to concentrate only on the shot in hand; never to get too far ahead mentally; the calming intake of breath – but they seemed of little value as he stood on the threshold of defeat.

Perhaps he really was destined to remain one of life's runners-up; always thereabouts but not quite there. In the last seven years he had been runner-up in thirty-one tournaments around the world and the problem had always been that his famous last-day charge, when he roared through the field with a fine score, lost its essential winning impact because he had played poorly in the opening rounds.

Yet even a good start this time and a fairly comfortable lead going into the final round had still not provided adequate protection as he faced the prospect of failure. This was the moment when Rodger Davis was about to find out the truth about himself – whether he was an outstanding player or a competent journeyman who would always stand just outside the spotlight.

When he reached the ball on the green he was disappointed. It had looked in the air as though it would finish closer but he was the best part of 30 feet from the hole. Des was nearer which was not good news because this Irishman thrived on inspiration and knew he was in control of this confrontation.

The awful reality at such a moment is that there is no way the next stroke can be avoided and that there is simply nothing left to do – no matter how dreadful the outcome – but to step up and trust the technique. That was the thinking anyway behind Rodger's work with the psychologist Noel Blundell, on developing the discipline of an inflexible pre-shot routine.

From the moment the club is taken from the bag, the routine never changes – the look at the target, the method of standing to the ball, glancing away down the line of fire, the actual contact. It had to be developed to such a degree that if routine was interrupted it must be started all over again. Its value was that the awe-some consequence of error was removed from awareness by the familiarity of the routine. Thus nothing must change. It was the same even with the putter.

So Davis had reached the inescapable moment when his future, his pride and his self-esteem hung on the putt that lay in front of him. And there was nothing he could do except hit the ball. And suddenly, he realized the ball was in motion, rolling, and therefore he must have struck it.

It still had 4 feet of its journey to complete when Davis realized it was on perfect line and could not miss. It was as though a thousand volts went through him. He felt the hairs on his neck stand up as he waited for the inevitable disappearance of the ball below ground.

It was enough to force a play-off as Smyth missed the mark. Davis had earned himself a reprieve yet both men knew that the slightest error would hand the title to the other in this sudden-death encounter. In extra time, they began to stalk each other, neither going for the outright winner but rather playing cautiously to see if the opponent would make a mistake.

At the third hole of their cat-and-mouse game it was Smyth who faltered with an errant tee shot out of bounds – at the notorious doglegged seventeenth on the West Course where so many fortunes and scorecards have been ruined.

It was the moment for Davis to play safe because a par-five would most certainly see him through to the title. But something in the thought process went awry and perhaps the treacherous gardens into which Smyth had struck his ball began to loom because Davis steered his one iron too far away and into the right-hand rough.

His next shot moved forward but still finished under trees. He hacked clear, now well aware that unbelievably he was handing the advantage back to Smyth who, from the depth of what had seemed inevitable defeat, began to show interest again, thinking all was not lost.

For a moment, it seemed that Davis was out of control; that the characteristically firm hold had taken over his life and golf had begun to weaken when he needed it most. What other explanation could there be as he saw his fourth shot race through the green?

Smyth was having his own troubles and knew that at best he could make par with his second ball which meant, with the penalty strokes, he was looking at an inevitable seven. Surely Davis would not allow this hole to be halved in the sort of double-bogey score that would make a duffer cringe.

Somewhere deep within Davis the resolution began to harden that this nonsense had to stop; that he would win this title for his wife, Pam, and for the children. All of them had come too far, made too many sacrifices for it all to fail now; even his pals, whose get-fit routine had helped him when he was at his lowest. All of them had played their part. It was a team effort and he would not let them down now.

This title was for them. And it was not going to get away. He chipped and he putted and he became PGA champion. He had joined the élite of world golf. But more importantly, he had restored his faith in himself. And he had discovered the most important truth which every aspiring professional hopes to learn about himself. It was not just a dream. The seeds of greatness really were within him all the time.

# CHAPTER ELEVEN

# Tony Jacklin and a debt of honour

There was a bet to be settled and, no matter how devastated he felt, Tony Jacklin had come to pay up. In an odd way, this silly ritual seemed to ease the pain.

He stepped out of his Rolls-Royce, clutching a bottle of champagne and walked in to the Greywalls Hotel, close by Muirfield's ninth green, then went in search of his friend, Tom Weiskopf, who had won the wager.

What had happened no more than an hour ago had been horrible and was still too fresh to make sense. The true enormity of the catastrophe had still not sunk in and that in itself was a mercy too.

He had been no more than a few minutes from winning the Open. No doubt about it. He should have been Open champion. Everybody thought he would be – even Trevino who now held the trophy in his place. But it was those last two holes – no, that seventeenth hole – where it had all changed and, though he could not know, where his life had changed too.

Throughout his life he had exuded confidence. His success was built on it. It

mattered more than his technique which at best was functional but not textbook. It was his indomitable spirit – that sureness that he would always win – that had seen him through.

In early days it had been regarded as arrogance and perhaps it was. He was the young assistant professional with the flashy red car and the gold lamé slacks who always drew attention to himself and, when he had broken through to become one of the richest sportsmen in Britain, he displayed the trappings of success – the Rolls-Royce and a country mansion in the west of England with a full complement of staff – in the grand style.

That supreme and impregnable self-belief had taken him to success on the American circuit where no British golfer since the missionary days of Harry Vardon, Ted Ray and company early in the century had ever triumphed. And he had reached the pinnacle by capturing the US Open title. Truly, there seemed to be no end to his success . . .

And yet here it was. Worse still, he had sensed – no, he believed – this was to be his title at Muirfield. There was an

Jacklin marched up Muirfield's final fairway still incapable of believing the Open title had slipped through his hands on the previous green and that Trevino was about to become champion. It was to change the rest of his life. *Colorsport* inevitability about the moment. Victory was about to become a reality and yet unthinkably it had not. A fluke chip shot into the hole from Trevino, compounded by his own silly errors as his mind went blank, had lost him the title. Trevino had not won it. The thing had been given away. The sureness that had guided his life was no longer there.

It was to be the start of a personal decline he could not halt and what made it worse was that he knew it was happening. What had vanished without trace was his self-belief; that absolute certainty that he was still a winner. Without it, he knew he was virtually powerless.

Perhaps he should blame Trevino. No. After all, everybody knew the American had a penchant for the outrageous shot and yet he, Jacklin, had held that title in his hand but could not close his fist. Time itself might ease that painful memory though he would come to learn in later years that what happened that day at Muirfield between Trevino and himself unquestionably ended his championship career.

It was a collapse that was to take him through all manner of turmoil – publicly and privately – and involved a long list of attempted cures from golf lessons to psychiatry and hypnosis, as well as a mild dabble with a quasi-religious sect. None truly worked and accordingly Jacklin, the most important figure in post-war European golf, faded into a personal wilderness – no longer good enough to command attention in his own right and too young to be elevated to the pomp and circumstance of elder statesmen.

There seemed simply nothing left for him to do except to live out his days as Yesterday's Hero, the man who had all-too-briefly reached the very top but could not stay there. And quite soon, the general verdict on his career was that while he had made his contribution to the game he had already become a half-remembered figure from its past.

When he was offered the job as captain of the Ryder Cup team, it had been a lifeline. It was a way back to the centre of the stage even if history had showed that the European team played the supporting role as inevitable losers to their American rivals. Yet Jacklin had shown during those brief glory years how the impossible – or the highly unlikely – could be achieved.

So be it. He would build a team of winners. If there was no place for him in the week-to-week arena of golf, then he would devote himself completely to this task. This would be more than just an honorary role for the three days of the match. Jacklin would turn it into a full-time task. He knew how important confidence had to be in any success story and he would strive to bring his team to the match against the Americans in a peak state of readiness.

He had been in too many losing teams and knew how the second-class image had sapped their self-esteem even before they started to play. It was a feeling of being cheap; more than that, there were the constant reminders of their inferiority. On one trip, the team had been obliged to rent their own headsets for the in-flight entertainment on the transatlantic journey. On another occasion, they had queued in 100 degree temperatures outside a shed and waited for it to open so that they could clear Customs and Immigration at St Louis.

They had been the poor relations and it was time to change. And Jacklin was the man to do it. On a personal level he had been associated with failure for too long. It was time for the sweet taste of success again. But the initial skirmishes of this match were not to be on the fairways. He fought behind closed doors for more say in the choice of the twelve-man team and settled on being allowed personally to pick the last three candidates. He had insisted that the team travelled and lived in first-class style and that they were given the best clothing and equipment money could buy. His argument was overwhelming. They had to feel good before they could play their best. Nobody disputed the point and Jacko won the day.

Moreover, he had recognized the richness of the emerging talent among the best players who would make up his team. But, first, there had been the task of persuading Seve Ballesteros to actually play again after his immense pride had been damaged when he was dropped from the previous match, apparently in retaliation to his demands for appearance money on tour, even though he had the British Open and US Masters to his credit and was one of the best golfers in the world.

What persuaded Seve more than any arguments was his respect for Jacklin, the man who had conquered the pressures of winning at the highest level; who had beaten the Americans and who was just as obsessed with doing it again if only to prove how good his men had become.

It was to be a formidable alliance and in 1983 in Florida they had almost swung it because they were to lose by only one point in such a closely fought struggle that Jack Nicklaus, the American skipper, had kissed the ground from which the winning shot had been made. It was as if he recognized the measure of the gathering European force and that they would not be subdued for much longer . . .

All that had passed and now here at The Belfry, two years on, Jacklin sensed the moment had come. And the ultimate irony of it all was that here, too, was the man who had ended his career all those years ago. Lee Trevino was in charge of the American team and he had arrived exuding his customary wisecracking confidence and perhaps, too, the familiar but quiet belief that even if the fight were to be a tough one, the outcome would be inevitable.

If any golfer in the world ought to make Jacklin feel second class, then it was Trevino. Maybe it was just the sense of being the junior partner; of playing the role of apprentice to a craftsman. And it was not just those haunting memories of Muirfield either. There had been their battle in the World Matchplay when Jacklin had become so tired of his endless banter and declared he did not want to speak during the match. Trevino had hit back, 'OK, don't talk. Just listen.' There seemed no way of winning and that day

# A ROUND TO REMEMBER

The old rivals - thirteen years after their Muirfield encounter - but now their qualities of leadership and strategy will decide the outcome of the 1985 Ryder Cup match at The Belfry. Jacklin was to prove himself to be a brilliant and successful captain. *Phil Sheldon*

he had lost despite playing some of the best golf of his life.

And yet here at The Belfry, Trevino's confident demeanour had begun to change and his appearances around the course became fewer as Jacklin's men had battled for two days against the American team to gain the upper hand. For Jacklin, it had been an extraordinary and unbroken scenario with no respite, not even after the matches had finished each day. He knew he needed to keep alive the collective mood and will of his men until it was all over.

He also knew – even if the Americans were not aware of it – that there was very little difference in ability among the top twelve players who had assembled from either side of the Atlantic to contest this match. He realized too that even if this were not the case, the vagaries of man-to-man encounters have always meant that any result is possible and that upsets – if that is what the unexpected win can be termed – sometimes happen.

Months earlier he had visited the Belfry Hotel and asked for a special room to be set aside where his team and their wives and girlfriends could meet each evening between matches. Jacklin wanted the mood of togetherness to be strong amongst his squad so that there was no coolness, no strangeness and no misunderstandings. It was to be an atmosphere in which every player could speak honestly and frankly about his own form. The team mattered above all else, and he needed each of them – and their loved ones – to believe that too.

The glaring paradox was that, even

in such a solitary and selfish pursuit as golf, the feeling of team spirit could win the day. He had seen that happen already back in 1969 when for no apparent reason a mood of confidence suddenly swept across the links of Royal Birkdale amongst his team-mates. It was almost telepathic although the roars of the partisan crowd had helped their mood. And yet suddenly they had all been inspired to new peaks of skill and had foiled an American victory.

Jacklin had told his men he wanted round-the-clock commitment. He had been the junior member in teams where as soon as play for the day was over, the stars said simply, 'Cheerio, see you all tomorrow morning.' Each team member went his own way or formed part of a little clique and the results showed on the fairways. That would not happen to Jacklin's men. They would live and work together – and for each other – until this was over, whatever the outcome. But after it – and because of it – they would have been brought closer together by the experience.

And yet there had been so many diversions, distractions, crises, panics and preoccupations to bring them to this moment where success – and against Trevino too – was almost within reach. Had he chosen the right three men to make up the last places in the team? The choice of Rivero had been criticized, but Jacklin knew the Spaniard played well at The Belfry and had won a tournament there.

But when he had paired him with Seve in the practice round, he knew immediately it was not working out. The young Spaniard was so much in awe of his famous partner that he could not play to his best. Jacklin switched them, during the practice and brought in little Manuel Pinero to play with Seve. It had been perfect chemistry because they would win three of their four partnership encounters.

He had told his team – and the press for that matter – that in the foursomes and fourball matches on the first two days he would play only the men who were on form because he knew he had to gather as many points as possible before the crucial last day singles series when everybody would play.

Until that moment, Jacklin would simply choose the right man for the job and omit others without explanation no matter how formidable the reputation of an individual might be. Yet on the Saturday morning, his heart sank as he read in the tabloid newspapers that Sandy Lyle, the reigning Open champion, was angry at being dropped from the first day fourball matches and growled unspecified threats about what he might do if dropped again.

It was peripheral stuff; meat and drink to the tabloids who regarded such sensationalism as an essential part of the grand occasion. Yet the episode had not damaged relationships or the mood within the group because Jacklin, after a lifetime of press dealings, knew that what was said was not always what was printed and that anyway Sandy, in his determination to do his best for the team, had every right to feel aggrieved at being dropped.

But the captain would have the last

word and that was the way it had been during those two crucial days when Nick Faldo, Ken Brown and Jose Rivero were obliged at times to sit on the sidelines because Jacklin said so. And yet all of them, particularly Jacklin and his backroom boys, Bernard Gallacher, Tommy Horton and Angel Gallardo, who had toured the course constantly watching each match, were suddenly struck by the exhilarating thought that the formula was working and that the Americans were becoming slightly unnerved.

Trevino had taken to wearing dark glasses. Perhaps his eyes were too expressive. The American wives began to complain that fans were hissing at them. Jacklin knew the only reason they were being hissed was because they were walking on the fairways and occasionally obstructing the views of no-nonsense Midlanders who had paid good money to watch the matches. But even the American players themselves were becoming rattled by the atmosphere. Hal Sutton had mouthed off about the bad sportsmanship of the crowds. True enough, a partisan cheer went up whenever an American mistake was made, but they were supposed to be supermen of world golf who were never bothered seriously by such things.

One stroke summed up what was happening to the American morale and seemed to capture the enormity of the moment and offer clear portent of what lay ahead for both teams on the final day. Craig Stadler had stood over a tiny putt on the last green to win his match against Langer and Lyle. Had it not

been for the win, it was short enough to have been conceded. But Stadler was obliged to perform the customary tap-in. He missed. And 25,000 fans had roared as he missed. The Americans were on the run.

And now it was the eve of the final day and Jacklin had to draw up his batting order and deploy his forces as best he could to protect or even increase their precious two-point lead. All his men had now played and were ready for the last push. Rivero had been brought in to partner Jose Maria Canizares in the foursomes that afternoon and scored one of the biggest winning margins in the history of the matches.

But now what? How to arrange this batting order? How could he outsmart Trevino, his old rival? What the American might do is lead from strength, pack his best men at the top of the draw in hopes of wiping out the two-point deficit by which they trailed Jacklin's men, and then leave the outcome to a frantic scuffle amongst the lower order.

Well, if he wanted to play it that way, Jacklin would pack proven men in the middle order to thwart any US attempt to over-run the singles. Trevino's best matchplayers would be who? Lanny Wadkins for sure. He had saved the 1983 match for them with that shot from the last fairway. Then maybe Stadler, determined to make amends for his error that had showed the true extent of US fears.

And the others? Ray Floyd, the most experienced of them all. But for sure, Trevino would attempt to protect the more vulnerable members of the team

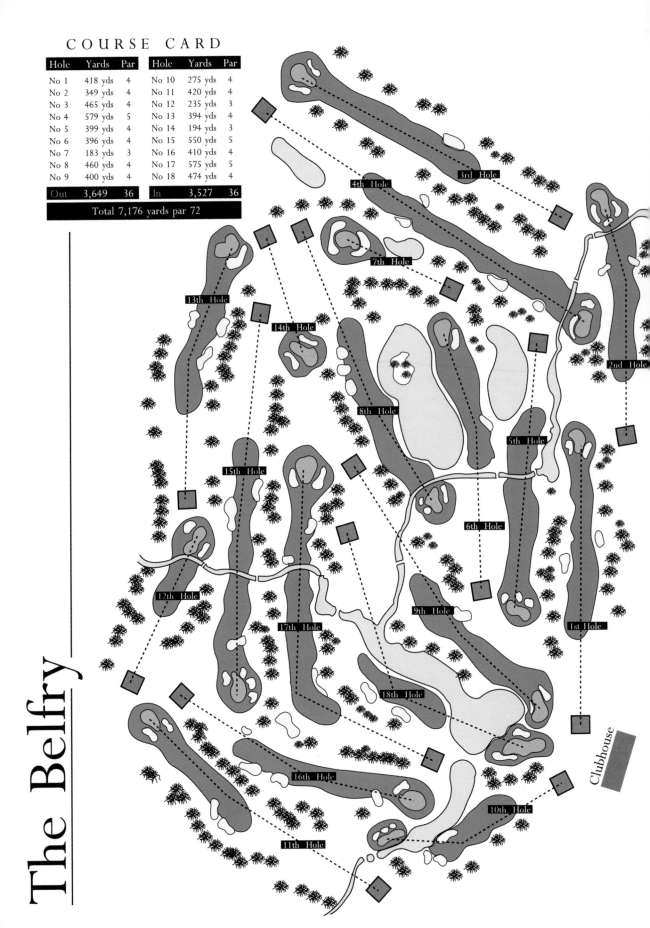

# The Belfry

## COURSE CARD

| Hole | Yards | Par | Hole | Yards | Par |
|------|-------|-----|------|-------|-----|
| No 1 | 418 yds | 4 | No 10 | 275 yds | 4 |
| No 2 | 349 yds | 4 | No 11 | 420 yds | 4 |
| No 3 | 465 yds | 4 | No 12 | 235 yds | 3 |
| No 4 | 579 yds | 5 | No 13 | 394 yds | 4 |
| No 5 | 399 yds | 4 | No 14 | 194 yds | 3 |
| No 6 | 396 yds | 4 | No 15 | 550 yds | 5 |
| No 7 | 183 yds | 3 | No 16 | 410 yds | 4 |
| No 8 | 460 yds | 4 | No 17 | 575 yds | 5 |
| No 9 | 400 yds | 4 | No 18 | 474 yds | 4 |
| Out | 3,649 | 36 | In | 3,527 | 36 |
| | Total 7,176 yards par 72 | | | | |

3rd Hole
4th Hole
7th Hole
13th Hole
14th Hole
8th Hole
2nd Hole
5th Hole
15th Hole
6th Hole
12th Hole
9th Hole
17th Hole
1st Hole
18th Hole
16th Hole
10th Hole
11th Hole
Clubhouse

– Peter Jacobsen, Hal Sutton, Andy North and Mark O'Meara – by hiding them in the middle order, and save the dependable anchor men – maybe Hubert Green, Fuzzy Zoeller and Curtis Strange – as tailenders.

That meant it was not worth using – perhaps wasting – a player in commanding form against Wadkins when at best he might salvage only a half-point. Best to save the top men to win points lower in the order and offer a sacrifice at the top. Pinero would undertake that job and yet Jacklin knew it was no use pushing all his best men into the lower places in the team because the match could have been lost by a weakened top end before they could take effect.

The good players had to come in quickly – Sandy Lyle, Ian Woosnam, Paul Way, Seve Ballesteros and Bernhard Langer – that's when it would be won. Heaven forbid that it should come down to a last match encounter. He wrote down his team and handed it over to officials. Then he received Trevino's batting order and his spirits rose. He had got it absolutely right.

Jacklin raced back to the special team room in the hotel and told Manuel Pinero, 'You're playing top and you've got Wadkins.' The little Spaniard jumped delightedly to his feet and said, 'He is the one I wanted.' As he read out the rest of the names, it was clear that his men were impatient to get on with the task.

That night Jacklin did not sleep well. But then that had been the disturbed pattern all week. Nor could he eat much and when he stood on the bathroom scales, he realized that he had lost 6lbs. But it was not entirely due to loss of appetite. The physical pace itself was punishing as he raced between matches to give his men support and worried when things went awry.

There were also those feelings of frustration that he could not do more to help the battle. He could only sit on the sidelines and play his part without a club in his hands. Then, too, there was the extraordinary awareness as the day dawned that the result lay there in wait for them; that by nightfall this battle would be concluded. But now they were being borne inevitably towards it. There was no turning back.

He took his place on the first tee to see them all launch their personal skirmishes that collectively would decide that day whether his efforts had been worthwhile or whether the attempt to break their image as the second-class citizens of golf had been simply a waste of time and effort. First, little Pinero. Then the diminutive Woosnam. Then Way, Ballesteros, Lyle, Langer, and on and on until Ken Brown struck the last tee shot and the battle was fully joined.

Trevino sat in his buggy and pondered, glancing occasionally at the scoreboard and waiting for his men to come back to the ninth hole, then watching them play from the tenth tee. Not Jacklin. This was his battle. And somehow the old memories of Trevino did not seem to matter anymore. It was an old score that did not matter either. There was a bigger prize within his grasp. In a sense this was the last part of a personal crusade whose origins he could not quite remember.

Throughout his career, Jacklin had done the best for himself and in the process of his success had helped others in his profession. But such altruism had never been the first objective but merely the by-product. Now it was different. At some moment, he had changed from being the leading soloist to the conductor; the maestro whose task and genius must find and inspire the best from others.

And yet that was still an artistry of the highest quality as he recognized the strengths and weaknesses of his men and manipulated and cajoled them. He thought as a professional; he knew exactly how they felt and how they suffered and as Jacklin sustained them, he was exhibiting his old talent and pushing it to its limits in altered form.

Yet there was more to it. He had sensed it and so had his wife, Vivienne. This lot were playing for him. All the propaganda about how their lives and fortunes would be made if they were to pull off this win had taken second place to a collective will to do it for Jacko. It was an emotion and esteem he had never before known. It made him feel rather vulnerable; that this love – for that is what it was – could touch him in this way.

He looked at the scoreboard and was astounded at its message. Pinero had sprung like a terrier at Wadkins and was savaging him. That uplifting news would appear on all the boards around the course and serve to inspire his men and strike gloom into the hearts of their rivals.

His team acknowledged what he had done for them and the debt they owed Jacklin and how too he had changed the face of European golf and given it world-wide prestige. *Phil Sheldon*

How odd that this should become not just a battle of skills but a war of nerves waged via the scoreboard. The news for the Americans got worse. Way, chirpy, cheeky and no more than a lad, was dealing the awesome Floyd a fierce mauling and had scampered four up after nine holes. That too was posted on the boards.

Jacklin needed five points to secure his victory. Those two – Pinero and Way – ought to be safe. But Seve was in trouble and three down to Tom Kite. If that match fell, its effect could boost American morale and spark off a revival.

Ballesteros knew it too, especially when he could see that young Way was letting his seemingly impregnable lead slip away to the wily Floyd. It was time for Seve to act even though there were only five holes of his match left against Kite. Before the American quite knew what had hit him, the Spaniard unleashed three birdies to level the encounter and earn the team a half-point.

Way had weathered the storm, or rather Floyd had inexplicably crumbled and attempted a shot of desperation from a bunker on the last hole to find the lake and lose two down. Now the points were tumbling towards Jacklin's men. Lyle delivered a victory. So too did the dependable Langer. And now only one point was needed of what remained to win the Ryder Cup for Europe.

But where? Sam Torrance came to the last hole on level terms with the US Open champion Andy North. The tension was overpowering and the American succumbed with a tee shot surrendered to the lake. Sam needed to detach himself from the pressure of the moment, switch off and allow his swing to work. And yet he could not. Instead he became inspired by the drama and drilled his approach safely to the green.

North knew he was a beaten man and that the cup was about to leave American hands. All Sam had to do was get the putt close for a safe tap-in and as he marched tearfully up the fairway he was greeted as a hero by the thousands who surrounded the green. In a second they fell silent as he hovered over his putt and then it was on its journey to the hole. The line was good and so too was the pace. Sam had judged both to perfection and the ball suddenly disappeared into the hole. He stood there, tears in his eyes, and holding his arms aloft. It was to be the enduring image of that 1985 victory.

'We've bloody done it!' cried Jacklin as he embraced the Scottish hero. But one of his team said, 'No. *You've* done it.' It was a moment of profound insight and perception amid the hysteria and jubilation. The celebrations would go on long into the night but first Jacklin waited until all his men had finished, even though their matches were matters of personal pride once the overall victory had been achieved.

It was time to reflect. Perhaps the horrors of Muirfield all those years ago had been essential to make this greater triumph happen now. It was not just the winning of the cup from the supermen; rather it was the realization that he had given European golf a collective awareness of and confidence in its own worth that extended beyond the few international stars.

All of them now knew they were good enough to stand comparison with anybody in the world. It was the doctrine by which Jacklin had lived his own life even before the days of personal glory. Even when he was an assistant professional working behind the counter at Potters Bar Golf Club pro shop this had been the conviction simply waiting for reality to catch up.

The game would never be the same again because of this moment. He had brought pride and status to it and in so doing changed the balance of power at its highest level. It would stand as the most important achievement of all and would never be forgotten because every subsequent victory would contain the seeds of what happened at The Belfry.

The next morning, Jacklin remembered there was something he wanted to say to Trevino. But it was too late. The despondent team had left and was en route in Concorde back across the Atlantic. 'I just wanted to tell him not to be too down-hearted, because he won't be the last losing American captain.' And no hard feelings about Muirfield either. Not now. Not after this.

# CHAPTER TWELVE

# Greg Norman and a late appointment

It was midnight and the policeman thought he heard a noise. In the darkness, he sensed there was somebody sitting in the grandstand, then suddenly realized it was the new champion clutching a bottle of champagne.

He understood and just smiled, then walked on. This was a private moment when more than just the glories of that day and its final moments on that eighteenth green would flood into Greg Norman's thoughts.

What was it Greg Norman had said when he collected the Open trophy a few hours earlier? 'At last I've got the monkey off my back.' Nobody doubted it. Until that moment of triumph, his life had been a crusade to balance the unfathomable equation of a talent that was good enough to win but somehow never quite did.

But there was more to it than that. It wasn't simply Norman's lack of success that caused the problem. It was more the monumental scale of his failures on the grand occasion when it seemed he had only to close his grip on a trophy already within his grasp.

And whenever it failed, he shrugged and consoled himself and others with the thought that there would be many more chances to come his way and that even Jack Nicklaus, the greatest golfer the world had ever seen, was a runner-up more times than he was ever a winner.

And while that statistic was inarguable it omitted the obvious addendum that neither had Big Jack snatched defeat from the jaws of victory with quite the same regularity as Norman.

Perhaps, after all, he was ill-suited to the myopic demands of golf at the very highest level. He was a cavalier, an adventurer. He took risks and he loved the exhilaration of attack. Why else did he hit the ball so hard? His way was to overpower the course as well as his opponents with his formidable prowess.

That, after all, was the nature of his character. He loved to fly in fighter planes. He had toyed with the idea of a career in the Australian air force. He loved fast cars – particularly Ferraris – and their speed was well known to the traffic cops around his Orlando home in Florida. But not even they could catch

There was a fury and zest about his style of play as though he always wanted to overpower a golf course. Most times it worked which is why the crowds flocked to see Norman. They were there in force at Turnberry in 1986.
*Phil Sheldon*

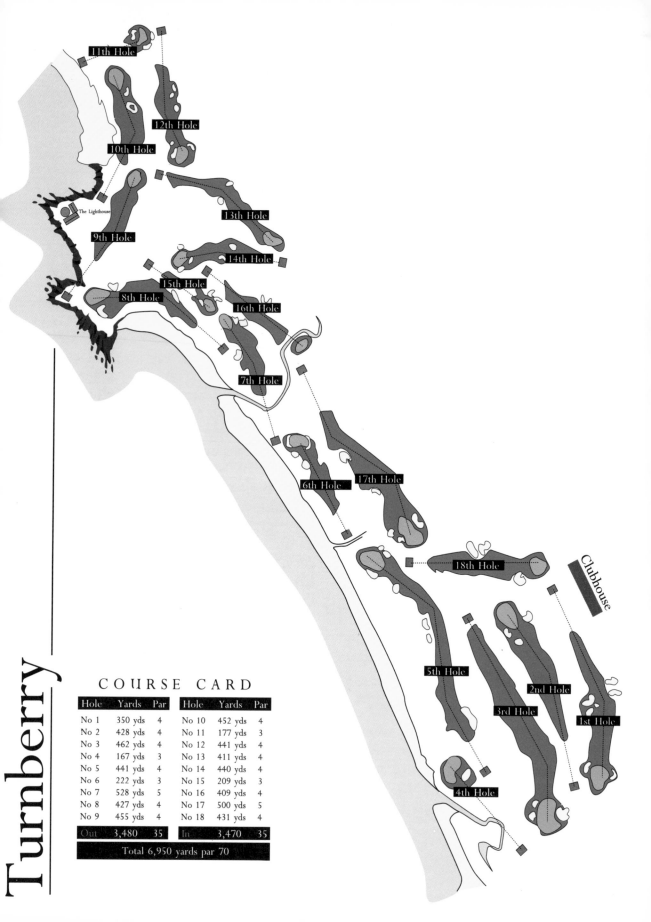

# Turnberry

11th Hole

12th Hole

10th Hole

The Lighthouse

9th Hole

13th Hole

14th Hole

15th Hole

8th Hole

16th Hole

7th Hole

6th Hole

17th Hole

18th Hole

Clubhouse

5th Hole

2nd Hole

3rd Hole

1st Hole

4th Hole

## COURSE CARD

| Hole | Yards | Par | Hole | Yards | Par |
|------|-------|-----|------|-------|-----|
| No 1 | 350 yds | 4 | No 10 | 452 yds | 4 |
| No 2 | 428 yds | 4 | No 11 | 177 yds | 3 |
| No 3 | 462 yds | 4 | No 12 | 441 yds | 4 |
| No 4 | 167 yds | 3 | No 13 | 411 yds | 4 |
| No 5 | 441 yds | 4 | No 14 | 440 yds | 4 |
| No 6 | 222 yds | 3 | No 15 | 209 yds | 3 |
| No 7 | 528 yds | 5 | No 16 | 409 yds | 4 |
| No 8 | 427 yds | 4 | No 17 | 500 yds | 5 |
| No 9 | 455 yds | 4 | No 18 | 431 yds | 4 |
| Out | 3,480 | 35 | In | 3,470 | 35 |
| Total 6,950 yards par 70 | | | | | |

him though they had warned his wife, Laura, that sooner or later they would.

There was an extraordinary paradox to all of it. His public image, his heroic style, was somehow larger than the real achievements on which it should have been based. It was out of proportion. There were champions who had won more than him but were lesser known.

That too simply added to the dilemma. Norman displayed an image which promised so much more. He was the macho man. He loved the great outdoors, went hunting in the Australian bush and even swam with sharks. His nickname – the Great White Shark – suggested the awe and respect he could command. He was toweringly tall, slim, flaxen-haired and had all the attributes of a Hollywood-style hero.

Yet he had chosen the fairways not the screen on which to perform. And he could not deliver. Or rather his failures had suggested that he could not fulfil completely the demands of the grand occasion even though he was skilful enough to be a constant contender.

In all of this, there is of course a knack to be learned. Most often, it is acquired and best retained through failure, which brings its own sense of self-knowledge of how outside forces and the drama of the moment take effect and what is needed to control them.

Moreover, Norman was not the first golfer of talent to face the task of trying to confirm his ability with a major title. The game is built on such heroes because the victory itself, when it came, underlined this greater triumph of self-belief.

In the 1930s the public expectation focused on Henry Cotton to win the British Open became so great and personally demanding that it contributed to his decision to live in another country to escape the pressures. Within a year he had become Open champion, while on a visit from Belgium.

But there was another code by which all the great players lived and it had been defined by the venerable Gene Sarazen when he reflected, 'At the end of your career they don't ask how much money you've made, they just want to know how many majors you won.'

That truly was the big quest because

He had led in both the US Masters and US Open going into the last round and had lost. Norman faced the same fears again as he led on the final day at Turnberry. *Phil Sheldon*

money was no problem for Norman. He had been showered with contracts because he had burst upon a lacklustre American scene in the wake of Arnold Palmer, Jack Nicklaus and Lee Trevino, in an era when the top players had an assembly-line similarity and could only be distinguished by the names of their sun vizors.

He was also capable of the most astounding golf. He played with a flair and pace that had not been seen since Arnold Palmer was at his peak. It was his customary style of play. Norman could not dig in, play safe, or find wise and manageable routes around a golf course.

To him, it had to be tackled head-on and that was the reason for his top box-office appeal with American fans and why he was such a rich earner. The fans liked too that he had made his home on American soil and dedicated himself to the US game, unlike other visiting overseas marauders who simply came for the money and left.

And yet the trouble with a talent that flares is that it can choose the wrong moments to ignite; or rather, not the appropriate occasion when the titles and prizes involved bear obvious evidence of a champion.

That realization prompted another fear; that he could grace international golf for a period during the twentieth century and become its brightest and most exciting star wherever he played in the world, yet would be forgotten by ensuing generations simply because there was no evidence of him in the championship record books. Even his money earnings would eventually pale into insignificance as more cash was offered in events.

There was compelling evidence of this harsh fact of life already, in that Ben Hogan, unquestionably the greatest golfer of his generation and the man by whom all others judged themselves, was ranked no higher than 300th in the all-time money winners list.

For a lifetime in which he collected sixty-two titles and set the modern Grand Slam of winning three major titles in a season, Hogan had earned $207,779. Yet just in that current season Norman had already earned double that amount.

If successful golf was just a question of earning money then Hogan would soon be forgotten. But the truth was that achievement was the true measure and Hogan's legend would stand untouched for all time, particularly because nobody had subsequently matched his slam of the US Masters, the US Open and the British Open in the summer of 1953.

He missed playing in the American PGA championship that year, and with it the chance of a 'full house' of titles, for various reasons, including the time spent travelling back from the British Open and his known reluctance to play thirty-six holes a day because of the strain imposed on his legs that had never fully recovered from a car accident four years earlier.

But Norman? The irony was that his season could well be remembered as a Grand Slam of failure and perhaps was best forgotten. He had led going into the final round of the US Masters at Augusta and at the US Open at Winged Foot. And he had lost both.

So it was that he came to the last round of the British Open at Turnberry in the lead once again, and there were those who had waited around the first tee for him to play who wondered whether another near-miss might not shatter his confidence beyond repair.

In the process of winning there is always a sense of destiny; a conviction that, come what may, things will turn out right. It is always felt, but rarely revealed by most champions. Seve Ballesteros called it 'destino'. Max Faulkner, the flamboyant 1951 British Open champion, felt it as a force which seemed to fill his entire body.

It may be best perceived in its absence or when it falters. In truth it was probably not Lee Trevino's historic chip shot at Muirfield in 1972 that ended Tony Jacklin's competitive career, but rather the fact that the Englishman's utter certainty that he himself was about to win had been crushed. Nothing could ever be the same again. He could no longer trust that sureness – if indeed it would ever return.

For Norman that conviction had begun to seep away at the beginning of the season when he stood on the final tee at Augusta, tied for the lead with Jack Nicklaus and knowing he needed a birdie to become champion or at worse a par four to force a play-off.

He had attacked this uphill hole all week, by taking a driver from the tee and aiming on the left-hand fairway bunker with just enough fade to let the ball drift back into the middle of the fairway. But this time he stepped out of character and selected a cautious three wood. Not bad, however, because he was in the fairway but now required a longer iron to reach the green.

The four iron was ballooned wide and right of the green and into the gallery. Afterwards he could find some technical reason – some error of weight transference – for this errant shot. But it left him an awesome stroke from the bank just to manoeuvre the ball to the green in the hope of stopping it somewhere close to the hole.

This was a crisis of his own making and it was about to become much deeper as he was now required to summon the best of his skills to keep his hopes alive when only minutes ago he had been engrossed only with thoughts of winning. Now he needed a miracle stroke. The recovery was good, very good, but always out of control and ran 16 feet past the hole.

He stood over the putt and fought a losing battle with his own touch and judgement. The ball ran 4 feet past and Norman had seen another chance of glory slip by. Nicklaus knew he had won because of that mistake. But he took his sixth title just the same.

Would he have played that hole differently had it not been Jack Nicklaus he was trying to beat? Had the Golden Bear cast his giant shadow over Norman as he had done to most of the younger challengers who came his way?

Perhaps he admired the man too much. They were friends and neighbours in Florida and though Nicklaus's manner

# A ROUND TO REMEMBER

The shot that was to cost Norman his chance of the 1986 US Masters. Under pressure, the approach is pushed wide of the target and he misses the chance to force a play-off with his close friend and mentor, Jack Nicklaus. *Phil Sheldon*

was always friendly it was impossible to forget his phenomenal record of twenty major titles and the degree of talent and will-power it had taken.

Perhaps in a sense Norman had cast himself as the junior partner, the avid learner, and when the moment had arrived for him to deliver a personal blow to the elder craftsman, he had been too deferential to step out of place.

Whatever, it was time for Norman to forget. But he could not, or more precisely, was not allowed to when he arrived at Shinnecock Hills in New York a couple of months later for the US Open. On that third day he had let slip a five-stroke lead and a boisterous and drunk spectator had shouted, 'Norman, you're choking!'

He should have ignored the jibe but instead walked over to the man and growled, 'If you want to say something to me, say it to me after this round when I can do something about it.' Not that they came to blows or even met again and by the time he had taken the lead at the start of the final round, the incident had been forgotten. Yet, once again, Norman was to find himself fighting his rivals at close quarters as thirteen of them were covered by four strokes. Was there enough space for him to flourish? Sufficient room for his customary flair?

His confidence and that special sense of destiny had vanished. His approach shot to Shinnecock's first green was so tentative that the ball did not reach the putting surface. He began to pull shots wide of the target and was to plunge into oblivion. He bogeyed five out of eight holes while Raymond Floyd marched on

to become champion.

Now at Turnberry he had reached that sombre threshold again, with memories of what had happened to him at the other two championships still lingering. This was going to be another tight fight too. Just like the others.

He had evidence of how well he could play because he had produced an astounding display of shot-making and power golf over the links beside the Firth of Clyde and reduced it to 63 strokes in the second round and might well have earned a 60 but for three careless bogeys.

What made that performance all the more impressive was that Turnberry had prompted a chorus of complaints – from Norman as well – about the narrowness of its fairways and the height of its rough. Tom Watson, who had won the Open there in an epic duel with Jack Nicklaus in 1977, complained that in a cross-wind some holes became virtually unplayable.

Norman himself openly questioned whether players would suffer injuries to arms and backs as they tried to play recovery strokes from long grass and whether any legal action for damages could be taken against the Royal and Ancient Club of St Andrews, which organizes the championship, for the manner in which its officials had set up the course.

And yet he had overpowered Turnberry with that 63 in the smash-and-grab manner that he loved to play and at which he was the game's master. They told him after he three-putted the last green that he was close to a record but he was not bothered. He was not interested in short-term gains in the record book.

He even weathered the furious storm which swept across the links on the third day and by the end of it found himself one stroke clear of the Japanese professional, Tommy Nakajima, with whom he would be partnered in the final round.

That evening up in the Turnberry Hotel, the other professionals knew the tensions and demons that would now assail Norman as once again he led a major championship yet had to fight the memories of how the other two had been fumbled.

There were other damaging memories too. Back in 1984, he had struggled to make a miraculous four on the last hole of the US Open at Winged Foot that earned him a place in the play-off with Fuzzy Zoeller. That time, from the middle of the fairway, he had hit his approach into the grandstands yet had still holed an outrageous putt for his par.

Then too it had been a crisis of his own making. The errant shot under pressure followed by the inspired recovery. He was convinced that he never backed away from a crucial shot. That fan at Shinnecock had got it wrong. He was not afraid. That may have been the trouble. Perhaps he attacked too blindly. Maybe the technique was flawed. There was much to consider.

In the restaurant of the Turnberry Hotel, Jack Nicklaus spotted Norman, went over to his table and sat down. Then he said very quietly, 'Nobody in the world wants you to win tomorrow more than I do. You've got all that it needs to win. Just concentrate on the pressure of your grip on the club. That will dictate your tempo.'

As Nicklaus spoke, the words seemed to lift Norman's spirits so that he was no longer apprehensive. The best golfer in the world had just expressed complete faith in his ability to become a champion.

So it was that he presented himself at the first tee the next afternoon after passing the hours impatiently while waiting for his starting time. Then, suddenly, it had begun and Norman was walking down the fairway after his golf ball.

In such moments the time taken to walk between shots simply disappears so that the golfer is confronted simply with a succession of ever-changing predicaments – rather like a series of picture slides – and is unaware of all else.

Norman was safely on the first green but Nakajima, his main threat, missed, then chipped quite close but inexplicably three-putted. Norman suddenly realized he was now three strokes clear after only one hole had been played.

Was it really going to be this easy? The same question occurred again when he bunkered his approach to the third green with an awkward four iron then punched his recovery 25 yards straight into the hole for a birdie. Now he was four ahead.

Norman was now hurrying to keep his appointment with the trophy. His stride lengthened and there was an urgency about his whole demeanour. Nothing would stand in his way nor would anything go wrong for him this day. He selected a four iron to play into the eighth green and deposited the ball 5 feet from the flagstick for another birdie.

He thought to himself, 'OK fellows, I've just shut the gate. It's mine.' And yet his caddie, Pete Bender, was more cautious. He could see that Norman was almost running between strokes and that, in this high state of excitement, he might make all manner of unthinking errors.

He had warned him earlier, 'I can see that you are walking very fast. I want you to walk at the same speed as I do.' Norman knew he must do as he was told because he could not get the necessary perspective on himself to sense such errors.

His stroke to the ninth green was wayward and misjudged and finished in the grandstands. An official led him to a designated dropping zone which had been marked by white paint and Norman noticed that it was nearer to the hole than the point at which his ball came to rest. So too did Nakajima.

The Japanese professional instantly questioned the correctness of such a move and while Norman himself was surprised that a fundamental tenet of golf had been contravened in this way, it nevertheless had the blessing of the ruling body and he was happy to comply. He chipped to 6 feet and saved his par four.

A quick look at the scoreboard informed him he was now five strokes clear of his nearest rivals, Nakajima and Ian Woosnam, a rising young star on the European circuit. From now on Norman knew that the only threat to his chance of victory would be his own imperfections. Yet this was one battle that, after all the previous failures, he intended to win.

Even then he could not be quite sure. He had seen disasters grow from the most innocent and apparently harmless of beginnings. There was still time for total crisis especially when he dropped a stroke for bogey five on the eleventh hole. But then that was the trouble with a big lead. Even the smallest error assumes terrifying proportions and prompts fears of decline.

He could not sit on his lead. He still needed to attack. Anyway it was not in his nature to coast and play safe. When he tried that tactic in the US Masters earlier in the year, he had lost the title. He needed to press on and keep trying to force birdies from what remained of the championship.

He drilled a seven iron from the rough and watched as the ball soared on target for the flagstick, then collided with it to finish 3 feet away. The putt was a formality.

Even the remaining holes began to blur as he caught sight of the clubhouse and the grandstands beside the last green and knew it was almost over. But he still had to remain focused on the task in front of him. One stroke at a time and no thoughts about what was to come.

Dave Thomas, the powerful Welsh professional, used to tell the cautionary tale of his 1966 challenge for the Open championship at Muirfield: he had found himself in the lead over the closing holes and let his thoughts stray to the highly expensive sports car he would be able to buy himself with first prize money. It did not happen because he lost out to Jack Nicklaus.

Now Norman was in crisis. His tee shot to the long seventeenth had been blocked wildly into the hills and there followed an anxious march then search by player and caddie to find the ball. Surely it could not go wrong now.

When he found it, Norman knew he must hack the ball back to the fairway with a sand wedge because he must now protect what must soon be his prize. In any case he knew he would need no more than a six iron up the valley to the green and that he could still escape with par.

The first part of the plan worked well enough. He lobbed the ball back into play then drilled the six iron to the putting surface. But then he was astounded at the eerie feeling that came over him as he stood on the green with the putter in his hands.

He was only 5 feet away from the hole and all outside threats to his success had virtually disappeared but he suddenly confessed to his caddie, 'Pete, my mind has gone dead. I can't see the hole. Tell me what the line is and how hard to hit it.'

Norman seemed to have no idea what he was doing. The putt was charged 4 feet past. There had been no judgement nor skill involved in the stroke and the crowd were aghast. He could now only trust to instinct and rely on his technique and this time the ball dropped.

The last hole passed as if in a dream. He was hitting, marching, being cheered by thousands, then pursued by the horde breaking through the barriers and then he was putting, picking the ball from the hole and raising his arms in jubilation as the new champion . . .

. . . And now in the darkness it was time to dwell on it all; to reflect that he had earned his niche in the history of the game and would never be forgotten no matter what else lay in store for him, and no matter how many near-misses his prodigious talent brought him.

Though he did not know it, that single thought would sustain him through a succession of heartbreaks still waiting to come in his playing career. But mercifully that night, there was no crystal ball and he was alone with the knowledge that at last he had become the champion everybody knew he should have been. Even Jack Nicklaus.

# CHAPTER THIRTEEN

# Jack Nicklaus and the day the bear got loose

The newspaper cutting had been stuck to the fridge door so that sooner or later Nicklaus would see it and get the message. His career was over and the great deeds were done. It was time to settle back and become a famous name in the history books.

The precise tone was more abrasive. He was finished, washed-up, and through. The columnist had pulled no punches in his unequivocal judgement of the life and times of Big Jack and the arguments were compelling.

Here was a man in his middle years and edging towards fifty. His back hurt. He was short-sighted. He was colour blind too, but that had not seemed to be a hindrance. His career had been the stuff of legends but now it had simply run out of purpose.

He was no longer the Golden Bear who had cast such fear into his rivals that whenever he played they assumed they had to compete for second place unless he had a bad day. Not any more. All they perceived now was an ageing millionaire, the father of five grown-up children who was not the force he used to be.

When Nicklaus arrived in the house he had rented in Augusta for the US Masters that year, he was well aware of the predicament even if he declined to admit to it in public. His business career – especially his golf course design work around the world – had taken more and more control.

But that was his nature. He needed to be totally involved in all aspects of his commercial empire. He had to be at the centre and know exactly what was going on and, after consultation, make the decisions. It was one of the reasons he had decided to dispense with the expert service of a sports agent.

And yet, with the customary highs and lows of trading and financial matters, such involvement had brought its own worries and concerns which had served to distract him from his primary purpose of playing competitive golf better than anyone else of his time.

Such matters were on his mind when he arrived at Augusta and there were unavoidable signs that perhaps after all this time in a career spanning twenty-six years, his winning touch had gone.

His talent was beyond dispute. But the American public saw Jack initially as the threat to their beloved Arnie Palmer and were hostile. Through his sustained success, Nicklaus earned their respect and affection. *Bob Thomas*

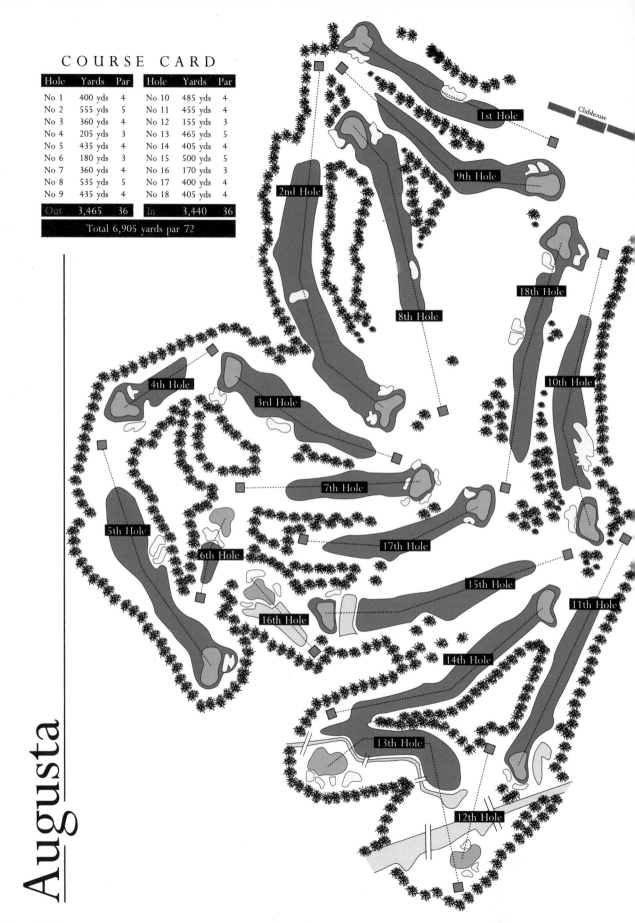

COURSE CARD

| Hole | Yards | Par | Hole | Yards | Par |
|------|-------|-----|------|-------|-----|
| No 1 | 400 yds | 4 | No 10 | 485 yds | 4 |
| No 2 | 555 yds | 5 | No 11 | 455 yds | 4 |
| No 3 | 360 yds | 4 | No 12 | 155 yds | 3 |
| No 4 | 205 yds | 3 | No 13 | 465 yds | 5 |
| No 5 | 435 yds | 4 | No 14 | 405 yds | 4 |
| No 6 | 180 yds | 3 | No 15 | 500 yds | 5 |
| No 7 | 360 yds | 4 | No 16 | 170 yds | 3 |
| No 8 | 535 yds | 5 | No 17 | 400 yds | 4 |
| No 9 | 435 yds | 4 | No 18 | 405 yds | 4 |
| Out | 3,465 | 36 | In | 3,440 | 36 |

Total 6,905 yards par 72

Clubhouse

1st Hole
2nd Hole
3rd Hole
4th Hole
5th Hole
6th Hole
7th Hole
8th Hole
9th Hole
10th Hole
11th Hole
12th Hole
13th Hole
14th Hole
15th Hole
16th Hole
17th Hole
18th Hole

Augusta

Worse still, he could no longer keep pace with the younger players. He was ranked among the no-hopers in 160th place in the money list. He had played only seven events, had failed to finish in four and been placed no higher than thirty-ninth in the others.

Time to quit? Perhaps the process had happened anyway and he did not know it. One of his pals had pinned the press cutting to the door of the fridge. It was typical of their hard-edged humour anyway. Those close to Nicklaus never knew what practical joke might happen next – a lorry load of manure in the front drive or a tankful of fish in their pool. He required sturdy company around him even if he was often on the receiving end.

But there was more to it than just an impish dig at his famous ego. It hid the thought that the great strength of his career had been his motivation and if it could be stirred vigorously once again, there might just be a chance he could summon his playing powers to their former pitch.

But this was the Era of the Young Hero. Seve Ballesteros and Greg Norman commanded the centre of the stage and even Tom Watson, his main challenger of another time, had been pushed to one side by these thrusting young superstars who now displayed the sort of rightful conceit and arrogance with which he himself had dominated the game for more than twenty years.

For goodness sake, he had a son, Jackie, almost as old as these heroes and even he had ambitions as a professional golfer. His second son, Steve, was

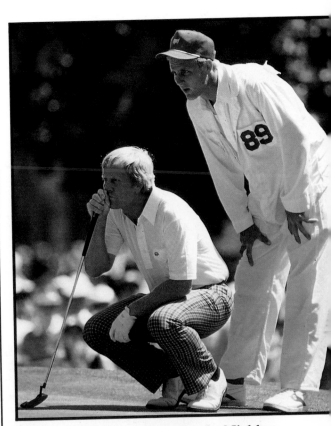

a high-powered executive in the Nicklaus organization. In fact, wherever Big Jack looked, he could find reminders that he was of another age and that it was now the turn of others to dominate.

And yet he still loved the atmosphere of tournament golf and more than anything he could not forget the feeling of involvement in the pursuit of victory even if he did not always achieve it. There was no greater thrill than to be three holes from home and need a birdie and two pars to win. That was the purpose of it all and no matter how important the business empire might seem, with his factories, fashion wear, books, films, course designs and endorsements, that remained the reason for his life for so many years.

He turned championship golf into a family affair with eldest son Jackie working as his caddie in the 1986 US and second son Steve giving him advice by telephone. Nicklaus had become the new hero and proved there was enough room in public esteem for himself - and Arnie. *Phil Sheldon*

That year he had followed his customary routine and visited his mentor, Jack Grout, who had taught him since childhood, for a complete course of lessons. It was always the same each season even in the good times. He would ask the wise man to treat him as a beginner and teach him how to play golf again so that whatever faults had crept into his technique could be eliminated.

Young Jackie had helped this time too, with some tips on his chipping technique. It is a measure of a great player that he will take advice from any source if it helps and not question the wisdom of the person offering it. In any case, Jackie knew his father's game and had developed a professional eye for its strengths and weaknesses. Quite apart from family ties it was one of the main reasons Big Jack had asked the boy to caddie for him during the Masters that year.

He had always said he would compete only as long as he thought he had a chance of winning. But perhaps the advent of decline is not so obvious in golf as it might be in tennis where a man sees a serve fizz past him which in times past he would not only have reached, but returned with equal venom. True enough, the younger fellows ripped their drives past his, but it simply required a different strategy – a different club selection – to end up on the green in the same number of strokes.

Where their scores differed was in the putting and maybe this was the flaw; perhaps his ration of putts had been used up; his nerve no longer able to cope with the pressure that comes from knowing that a putt simply must be holed.

In times past there had been plenty of such pressure and he had revelled in it, while others crumbled under its demands. Perhaps that was the difference. He had always been meticulous in his preparations for the big occasion. He was one of the first golfers to chart golf courses, noting his own landmarks so that he knew precisely what distance was required on any strokes he had to play.

From childhood he had shown an inexhaustible work ethic. It may have come from what he called his Teutonic ancestors. The Nicklaus family had emigrated from the Alsace region in the middle of the nineteenth century. He would hit hundreds of golf balls each day at Scioto Golf Club in Columbus, Ohio, where he was a junior member and by the time he was thirteen he had broken 70. Within six years he was US Amateur champion and he had not yet turned professional when he almost scooped the US Open from Arnold Palmer.

Truly he was a prodigy, yet his self-assured brilliance and success found little favour with an American public which saw this overweight young golfer as a threat to their beloved Arnold Palmer, the small town boy who had become the folk hero of American sport.

For a time Big Jack was to be the most unpopular figure and faced the cruel ordeal of open hostility from fans at golf tournaments, some of whom would stand in the rough with placards bearing the message, 'Hit it here, Fats!' But Nicklaus would not succumb to such intimidation and had told Gary Player, 'The more they do that sort of thing, the more determined I am to win.'

And gradually he had worn them down or rather he had shown that there was enough room at the top for more than one star and that he would not supplant Arnie but succeed him at the top of the list. And there he stayed, unmoved and undisturbed for the lifetime of many of his contemporaries and even their successors.

What he had gained initially from his fellow professionals and golf fans was an awesome respect which began to transform itself into esteem and developed into affection so that he, too, became the people's hero – Big Jack, who for all his phenomenal achievements and wealth, remained essentially a devoted family man.

The strict observance of those two roles could at times become quite bizarre. During a tournament in Mexico City he had flown home to Florida each night in his personal jet to watch his children compete in a series of college basketball games. Then he had flown back after each match to get some sleep before the next round. That was the other side of fearsome Big Jack – the man who had attended the births of all his children and fainted every time.

His British fans perceived him as a rather aloof superman until two particular incidents changed their minds. In the last dramatic moments of the Ryder Cup match in 1969 he conceded a missable putt on Royal Birkdale's last green to Tony Jacklin, even though a miss could have given the American team victory. Big Jack made it clear that this was not the right way such a closely fought match should end. And the fans cheered him for his insight.

A year later they had roared their approval at St Andrews when he removed his sweater to drive his tee shot on to the last green of the Old Course to beat Doug Sanders in a play-off, and then threw his putter jubilantly in the air as the ball dropped. Nicklaus it seemed had joined the human race and experienced the same joys and doubts as the rest.

What greeted him as he played the last round of the 1972 Open at Muirfield was nothing short of love. They were willing him to win that title so that he could hold all three Majors at once. There were tears in his eyes when he failed yet he felt that day he had been swept along by their emotions and it was proof that he had served his time with his public and both he and they had formed an unbreakable bond.

Of course he had been written off in times past. Before that 1970 Open at St Andrews, he was said to be finished. But he had proved them wrong. He had ventured back from obscurity to win the 1980 US Open at Baltusrol after an interlude in which he himself began to wonder whether the secret of success had departed.

But this time it was different. He had told Lee Trevino how difficult it was to cope with the thought that people assumed that he was as good as he was ten years ago. He had confessed to Gary Player he was more preoccupied with business matters. And anyway there really was not much left to prove. Not with five US Masters titles, four US Opens, three British Opens and five PGAs to his credit as well as two US Amateurs. Nobody would ever again come close to that achievement.

And yet he had suddenly discovered a hint of that old determination even before he arrived that week at Augusta. He had worked excessively hard on the practice ground. And then he came home one day and told his wife, Barbara, 'I think I found the fellow out there I used to know. Me.' That was when those close to him really knew that all he needed was the motivation and the right breaks to become champion again.

Augusta, he knew, was a young man's course. It was long. It had fast greens. Its flagsticks were set on little knobs on those greens to strike terror into any faint heart. Everything about it suited the stamina and nerves of younger players. But nobody knew Augusta as intimately as Big Jack. Over the years he had practised incessantly upon it. They were old adversaries. He knew its moods, its subtleties and its treacheries.

His ideal practice was to play alone and throw the golf balls into the most awkward spots he could find – under trees, in bunkers – so that he would have visited the most outlandish parts of the course and armed with this knowledge would have more confidence when he came to play in the championship.

It is an essential and inevitable aspect of the days leading up to any championship that speculation on the form of players is the prime talking point and that week the future of Jack Nicklaus was top of the agenda. Quite apart from press reports about his decline, Nicklaus was also the subject of discussion on television when CBS commentator, Ken Venturi, had suggested it might be an appropriate moment for Jack to bow out and devote himself to all his diverse businesses.

Mercifully once the contest had started and there was real action to pursue, the future, or lack of it, as far as Big Jack was concerned was forgotten. He had made steady but unspectacular progress through the first two rounds amid the supporting acts, while Seve Ballesteros, Greg Norman and Tom Kite dominated the headlines and the television screens.

Even his 69 on the third day, while earning appreciative applause, was still regarded as merely a pleasant sideshow to the main event that would involve the new generation of stars. The Grand Old Man was having a little flourish – nothing more than that.

But by the end of that day, he was only three strokes behind the leading score. To him that did not matter as much as the number of players that were ahead of him. He counted eight and knew instantly he was in with a realistic chance. That evening the phone rang in his rented house. It was his second son, Steve, calling from Florida, 'Pops, what's it gonna take?'

Nicklaus pondered for a moment, 'It'll take 66 to tie. And 65 to win.' The young man came straight back, 'Well, Pops, go do it!' It was not so much a command as a clear act of faith. Father and son bade

# JACK NICKLAUS AND THE DAY THE BEAR GOT LOOSE

The moment which even Nicklaus suspected would never happen to him again. He raises his arms the new champion - the man who had defied middle age and all the best golfers in the world. *Phil Sheldon*

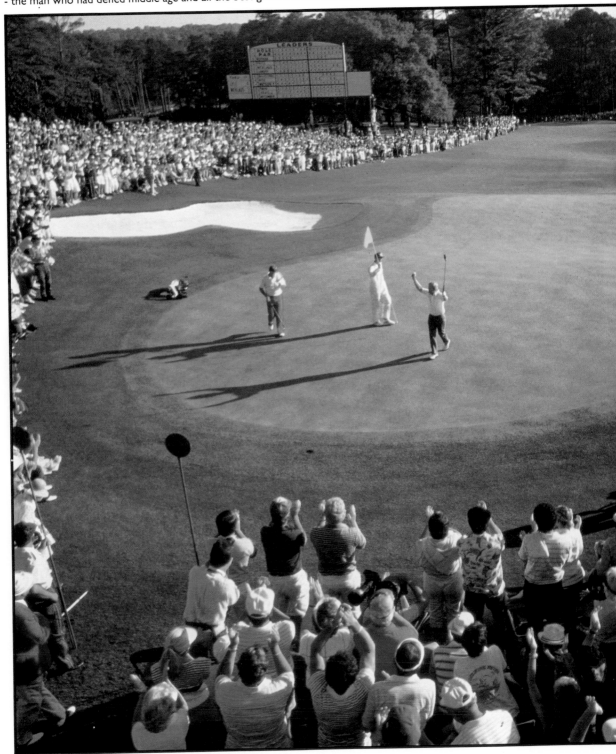

each other goodnight and put down their respective phones.

The last day of the Masters exudes an atmosphere of anticipation and suspense that is unmatched in the world of golf. There is the certainty of drama, disasters and triumphs, because that is the power it exerts upon the contenders. And, on such a day, the last nine holes of Augusta invariably prompt the best and the worst in performers who never dreamed they were capable of either extreme. In truth, it is the one arena in golf where the old cliché must never be forgotten for a moment: the game is never over until the last putt has dropped.

It was this thought that kept Nicklaus at his endeavours after an unremarkable start to that Sunday afternoon when it seemed as though he could force nothing from Augusta. There were occasional explosive cheers from other parts of the course, but after the predictable birdie down the hill of the long second hole and a vexing three putt on the fourth green, he was stuck at two under par.

The first sign of hope came as he punched his approach up the hill to the ninth green and the ball halted 11 feet above the hole. He crouched over the putt and the crowd around him fell silent. Suddenly there was a deafening roar back up the hill from the eighth green.

What he did not know was that Tom Kite had holed a wedge shot for an eagle three. Nicklaus stepped away, then crouched over the ball again but, almost at the moment he was about to strike, there was another roar from

the same area. It signalled a staggering riposte from Seve Ballesteros who had also chipped in for an eagle.

Once again Big Jack stepped away then he turned to the crowd and said, 'Let's see if we can get a roar here.' They laughed and were surprised because normally Big Jack never breaks that invisible barrier between himself and the crowds. He stood over the ball again and trickled it down into the hole for a birdie. The crowd obliged with a roar.

As he walked to the tenth tee, he sensed there was more to come and when he stood over a 25-footer on the next green there was no thought of simply getting the ball close for a safe par, he was utterly convinced the ball would drop. He could see the line and there was no doubt in his mind. Now he was four under par and he looked at the scoreboard. There were only six players ahead of him.

So it was he came upon Amen Corner, that notorious stretch at the far end of the course where so many potential success stories have been ruined but where brave men take their chances when they sense their time has come. Young Jackie was at his side but stayed silent as if knowing they were about to face a spectacular adventure.

He handed his father an eight iron as they sized up the approach to the eleventh green and the ball was delivered some 20 feet from the hole. Once again the old man hovered over the ball and knew – absolutely knew – he could not miss. Now he was five under par and there were only two men – Ballesteros and Norman – ahead of him. The word spread quickly. Big Jack was back.

He knew, as soon as the ball left the club on the twelfth tee, that he had launched it too far to the left and that it would finish at the back of the green. This was the moment of crisis when the temptation to protect what he had already earned in the way of score began to loom. Perhaps it had already caused this tentative stroke. His chip shot was just as unconvincing and he missed the putt which would have saved his par.

The error should have depressed him because he was now three strokes behind the lead but quite remarkably it had the opposite effect. From that moment, he knew beyond question that he had to be aggressive if he was going to win. He had to attack. There was no merit in caution, no glory in a tidy score.

He needed to overpower them all. And the old man realized it meant he must abandon caution, reach back to find a touch of that magic that had once made him all-conquering and attack the toughest stretch of golf terrain in all of golf. Moreover he had to hold off the best of the new generation, each of whom was equally convinced that this was to be their day – their prize.

He took a three wood from the next tee and chose a dangerous line close to the left-hand corner near the ditch. The trajectory frightened his son and when the ball came to rest he sighed, 'That was too close for a twenty-four-year-old heart!' In times past Jack would have taken the driver and aimed for the right side of the fairway and allowed the slope to bring the ball back to the middle.

Not now. He had to play within himself and battle this course as best he knew. That shot to the lower corner was risky but at least it gave him a flat stance and a better approach to the green. By now, he too was caught up in the emotion of this extraordinary moment as hundreds of fans flocked to see him in full cry – the man he used to be. He drilled the ball across the creek with a three iron and left himself close enough for two putts.

Nobody really looks for a birdie on the fourteenth because its green has too many savage sweeps and even the brave man is thankful to emerge with his par. But the long fifteenth across the water is quite another matter and Nicklaus surprised even himself with the length of the drive he launched down its fairway. It measured almost 300 yards and he wondered to Jackie what an eagle three on the hole might do for their chances. The son handed him a four iron and said quietly, 'Let's see it.'

As soon as the ball was airborne both men could see it fizzing towards the flagstick, not deflecting an inch either way in its flight. It plopped inches from the hole and ran on to finish 4 yards away. As Nicklaus walked to the green he looked at the scoreboard again. Seve had eagled the long thirteenth hole and was taking command of the day.

Father and son knew this putt had to drop if he was to stay in this chase though neither mentioned it. Big Jack stood over the ball but backed away when cheers broke out for another player on the adjacent sixteenth green. When he resumed there was no doubt about the outcome and he jumped in delight as the ball disappeared into the hole.

The short sixteenth is a daunting prospect when the pin is tucked close to the lake on the left but Nicklaus knew he could not afford to play safe because fate might never deal him this kind of golden chance again. In his prime he could always impose himself on an event. He was the man to beat in those days and always involved. But now he had to wait for the breaks and they had been few and far between. He could not afford to back away. He aimed at the flag and allowed the ball to take a line over the 170-yard stretch of water, then heard the roar of the crowd.

He knew it was close and when he got there, the ball was only 3 feet away, so that the birdie was almost a formality. At that moment, his fate was being helped by another extraordinary twist of fortune as Seve Ballesteros, who seemed to have the title in his pocket despite Big Jack's flourish, made the most astonishing error of judgement on the long fifteenth where a birdie four should have been routine.

He had boomed a drive down the fairway and pondered with his brother, Vicente, who was his caddie, whether to hit a four iron or five iron. He opted for an easy four iron and it was a fundamental mistake. In such moments of tension, the hardest stroke in the book is the one that requires finesse. A player is charged with so much excitement and adrenalin that the only safe strategy is to hit out hard. Seve knew as soon as he struck the ball he should have hammered it with his five iron. The ball plopped into the water and he struggled through to earn bogey six.

With that one disaster, Nicklaus had made up three strokes on the young Spaniard. And now the cheering would not stop. By the time Nicklaus reached the seventeenth tee, the fans were convinced he was to be their new champion. There were tears in his eyes. He blinked hard then sniffed. Son Jackie knew what was happening but dare not look at his father.

Nicklaus suddenly reminded himself that this contest still wasn't over and there was plenty of golf left to be played in which this title could be won or lost. His tee shot strayed slightly but still left him a safe stroke to the green and now he was no more than 10 feet from the hole. And he knew – he just knew as before – this ball had to drop because it marked the end of the birdie run. Nobody ever looks for a birdie up the last hole. The risks are too great.

He touched the putt into life then brandished his putter in the air as though it were a sword as the ball moved towards its target. He urged it on and on and on and the crowd roared to a gathering crescendo until it teetered to the edge and fell in. He had earned his birdie and he was nine under par.

He marched after a perfect drive up the hill of the last fairway and delivered the ball safely to the green and dutifully took two putts for an astounding homeward score of 30. Jackie embraced him because no matter what that score might or might not earn his father as the event unfolded, he had just seen him restored – perhaps momentarily – to his former glory. The old man had found the gift that everybody assumed had been stolen by the years.

And every step of the way on the last fairway he had been cheered by his fans who had joined him on the pilgrimage into the magical past and for whom he had rolled back the years as he showed them the Jack Nicklaus they too used to know. The joy was not just for his skilful display but for the resolute way he had held his ageing nerve and his fears in check.

He had delivered the score of 65 that he had told his son, Steve, would be good enough to win. Now he could only wait to see if he was correct or whether the others could catch him. Seve and Tom Kite were only a stroke behind with two holes to play. And Greg Norman was two behind as he stepped from the fifteenth green.

Seve was first to bow out of the fight as he bungled his chance on the seventeenth green and actually waved to the crowds as if acknowledging that he knew it was all over for him. But Kite came through knowing he still had a chance to tie on the last hole.

And Norman was on the move. Nicklaus could now only watch it all unfold on television and he saw that the Australian had earned his birdie two on the sixteenth and was eight under par but had hooked badly on the seventeenth to the edge of the adjacent seventh green and was blocked by two tall trees.

Yet, incredibly, he found a way through and over and the ball plunged obediently to the green and settled 4 yards from the hole. He took his time and casually stroked it home. He had just strung together four successive birdies and was tied with Nicklaus. A birdie on the last hole would make him Masters champion.

There is something in Norman's character that compels him to overpower golf courses and rivals. It is the only way of winning he knows. It is as though he needs to floor everybody with his sheer force so that they are either demoralized or intimidated by it. And now it was about to cost him the title.

The first mistake was to alter the tactics of the week and take a three wood from the tee instead of his customary driver. Perhaps he distrusted his adrenalin and feared he might reach the fairway bunker. Maybe he just wanted to have a full shot to the green that he could hit hard. Whatever, he was left with a four iron shot to the green and that was too much of a distance to be safe. He jumped at the ball far too quickly and was never quite in position to deliver full power and accuracy.

The ball drifted sickeningly away to the right of the green and up the embankment into the crowds. The birdie he needed to become champion was no longer a reality and instead he required all his skill to save par just to force Nicklaus into a play-off. The irony of this crisis was that he showed consummate skill in getting the ball off the hill to finish a few feet from the hole.

But those who saw him standing over the putt sensed that he knew he was already a beaten man and that this was another sad chapter in the saga of near-misses that were to dog his dashing career. The ball ran wide and Jack Nicklaus was US Masters champion . . . once again.

What had been proved? The revival of a legendary career? No, that was too much to ask. Unrealistic too. It was time to move on to those other important things that waited in his life to be achieved. Time to leave this stage to the new generation with just a reminder of what he had been.

He summed it up, 'I know I am not as good as I used to be. I just want to be occasionally as good as I used to be.' There was one last duty to perform before he left Augusta. He sought out the columnist who had written the disparaging piece that had adorned the fridge door all week. And he thanked him for stirring the Golden Bear into action. It meant the columnist had one more article to write . . . how he won the Masters for Big Jack.